Don Maclean

God Bless & Keep
laughing!

Don Maclean

To Christine
'Good Morning Sunday's greatest fan

DON MACLEAN

SMILING THROUGH

Judith Wigley

A LION BOOK

Published by
Lion Publishing plc
Sandy Lane West, Oxford, England
ISBN 0 7459 3350 5
Albatross Books Pty Ltd
PO Box 320, Sutherland, NSW 2232, Australia
ISBN 0 7324 1312 5

First edition 1996
10 9 8 7 6 5 4 3 2 1 0

A catalogue record for this book is available
from the British Library

Printed and bound in Great Britain
by Biddles of Guildford and Kings Lynn

CONTENTS

INTRODUCTION

I first met Don Maclean in 1993 at the City Varieties Theatre in Leeds although after three years of listening to him present 'Good Morning Sunday', I felt I already knew him. On this particular occasion we had been invited guests at the filming of BBC's 'Songs of Praise' 'panto special'. Cannon and Ball, Mary Millar and Dana were amongst the stars present. Don compèred the evening for the participating audience invited to sing hymns and 'Songs of Praise'. We sang and laughed until both throats and sides were sore. It was a lovely evening.

My husband and I are no strangers to theatre and particularly pantomime. Throughout his twenty-five years as chaplain to Bradford's Alhambra Theatre we've watched some of the finest performers and productions. But that night we felt we'd been in the presence of an experienced and most highly gifted all-round entertainer. It was clean, hilarious, cheeky and topical humour such as we hadn't encountered in a long time. We knew that Don had enjoyed a high profile on television some years previously but neither of us had tuned into those per-formances at the time. I began to realize that there was much more to this Sunday morning presenter than had met my eye.

I'd outgrown 'Crackerjack' by the time Don Maclean joined the team but I do recall the shrieks of laughter coming from the lounge where my much younger twin brothers tried to emulate the stage antics of Peter Glaze and Don Maclean. The 'Black and White Minstrels' of the seventies were never really part of my student scene although I remember my mother being very keen to watch this prime-time Saturday night television show. 'Good

Morning Sunday' was my first real introduction to this comic personality and initially, I was not amused by his performance.

Don had been invited to host 'Good Morning Sunday' for two weeks during the summer of 1990. We were on a family holiday in Cornwall at the time. I was grieving the loss of Roger Royle and felt quite incensed that the BBC had replaced a dignified Anglican clergyman of many years' experience with a half-cock comedian claiming some kind of Roman Catholic allegiance! At the time I could only thank God that Don Maclean was temporary. My husband pointed out that he was likely to be one of several presenters that the BBC would no doubt be trying out until they decided on a permanent replacement. He was right and I knew it would be some weeks or months before that permanent replacement would be announced. The thought of this 'bull in a china shop', as I had labelled him by then, sitting in the seat of an adorable, pastorally sensitive and gifted saint of a presenter horrified me. I was determined to influence this decision. I vowed the BBC would hear my opinions and spent many hours lying on the beach composing my letter to the Head of Religious Broadcasting. As was often the case, since I had four children and a busy vicarage to contend with, my desire to influence the powers that be never got further than my beach compositions. In this case I am thankful.

By now you will be forgiven for asking the inevitable question, 'Why write a book about a man you never saw on television or stage and disliked on radio?' Well, I had failed to find a suitable replacement for my early-morning companion as I prepared lunch for endless vicarage guests and watched my husband flit in and out from early morning services of Holy Communion. (If ever BBC religious broadcasting carry out a survey of their viewers and listeners I can guarantee a surprising high percentage of clergy families amongst their numbers.) Having scanned local radio stations and found nothing to my liking, I quickly tired of Radio 4's political and news approach to their 'Sunday' programme. So I continued to listen to 'Good Morning Sunday'.

It wasn't very many weeks before I found myself setting the alarm earlier in order to catch the first part of the programme that I had usually been happy to miss. There was something very likeable, open, honest and refreshing about this man's style of presentation that was intriguing me. The most striking feature was his ordinariness: no masks or pretence—he said what he felt and thought without apology or embarrassment. Week by week Don drew from his guests equally real, honest and open responses exposing people with human faces that for some had been shaded by fame and fortune. He also attracted response from his listening audience, entering into topical debates on subjects affecting a wide range of issues relating to faith and church life, in which those with little or no faith felt happy to participate. For me the programme was turning into a fascinating weekly education into the attitudes and opinions of a large chunk of the nation towards faith and the church. This I could not afford to miss.

That night in December 1993 at Leeds City Varieties I dared to tell Don my early objections to his performance. I watched his warm eyes communicate sadness, his sensitive nature showed a flash of hurt and I began to wonder whether I'd done the right thing. Seemingly I hadn't been the only one with such thoughts and feelings in the early days of his presenting the show. But Don Maclean is not frightened of facing criticism, only concerned not to offend or hurt. As I quickly moved from criticism into praise and admiration for his skill and ability in presenting this now weekly two-hour show he thanked me with a humility rarely encountered in showbiz circles. 'If playing good old Radio 2 music and telling a few folk that God loves them helps some to believe, then I'm happy,' was his reply.

Since then it has been my joy and privilege to get to know Don and the Maclean family a lot better. They are inseparable. If you chose to write about Don, then you write about them all—

and they all share his energetic personality and radiant smile. For those who haven't had that privilege, I hope that you'll meet Don Maclean in the pages of this book. He is warm and friendly, tremendous fun, full of faith in God and the greatest advocate of marriage and family life that I've met in a long time. I hope you enjoy the meeting.

Judith Wigley

1
Family Roots

At some time or other we've probably all used the well-known phrase, 'You're a born comedian!' or 'You're a born entertainer'. But when you stop to think about it, no one is actually 'born' either of these things. In the same way, scientists are not born scientists or cooks, cooks. It would be more accurate to say that they *become* them. So we may well wonder exactly how comedians become comedians or entertainers, entertainers. Who or what gives them their sense of humour and desire to perform? No doubt there are as many different answers to these questions as there are individuals in this rare and talented group of people. Each story is unique and Don Maclean's is no exception, not least because in recent years he has successfully combined two worlds that traditionally sit uncomfortably with each other—the worlds of entertainment and religious broadcasting.

Some experts tell us the early influences on our lives can have the strongest pull of all. They may determine the way we look at life, dictate our decisions or even lay down the direction in which we go. Few of us are completely unaffected by our roots. Don's life began in Sparkbrook, Birmingham on 11 March 1943. It has already spanned over fifty years, more than thirty of which have been spent in the world of show business. These working years have been a carefully navigated journey, with its fair share of hills and valleys, plateaus and plains. Throughout, there has never been any attempt to cover up where it all began.

Don proudly acknowledges the place and people that provided the foundations for what has become a happy and fulfilling career, full of richness and variety.

Sparkbrook in Birmingham lies on the main A34 Stratford to Birmingham road, at the city centre end. Two other famous comedians started out from the very same point. Some might suggest that in itself as an early influential factor! The late Sid Field put Birmingham on the map long before Don was born and Tony Hancock followed some years later. Whilst both men were proud to be 'Brummies', neither continued to live there, each gravitating towards London, the heart of the entertainment world. The young Don Maclean was clearly influenced by their humour but not in their decision to leave their home city. Sparkbrook was home for over twenty-three years and provided the foundation for a happy, secure childhood and a base from which he was to launch his career.

Charles and Rosina Maclean's terraced house had a long thin back garden and a front door that opened straight on to Ombersley Road. It was small but adequate, rich in its provision of security and home-made comfort. Born towards the end of the Second World War Don recalls fond memories of his early childhood, playing happily on the street, creating hours of his own entertainment and enjoying outings to the local park and cinema. Among his earliest memories is the sight of bunting flying between the terraced houses, tables laden with food lining the streets and an atmosphere of jubilance as adults and children gathered together to celebrate V.E. Day. The rationing of war years and the absence of certain foodstuffs, particularly meat, was never a hardship to this small boy who delighted in eating dehydrated potatoes and dried eggs. Such was his enjoyment of the healthy wartime diet, Don—with a few memorable exceptions—began and continued life as a vegetarian.

Charles Maclean was of Scottish descent, fourth in a line of five children, his parents having moved from Glasgow before the First World War. As a child Don's grandmother had lived in

John Knox Street in Glasgow's city centre and worked on the huge ocean liners fitting cane bottoms into cabin bunks. Her husband and his father, Don's great-grandfather, ran a business making Windsor chairs in the front room of the family's terraced house in Succhiehall Street. These small family houses were later demolished and have since become the site of the city's large Woolworths store. The depression on the Clyde caused many to leave the city in search of employment. The Macleans, unlike others, did not choose one of the other major Northern shipbuilding towns but Birmingham, where they continued to earn a living through making Windsor chairs. It was here that the eldest son, Charles Maclean, met his future wife.

Rosina Field was one of five children from a strongly Roman Catholic family in the Sparkbrook/Moseley area of Birmingham. Her father and brothers worked buying and selling fish at the Bell Street wholesale market. Don never knew his grandfather, who died prematurely at the age of forty-one, but shared in his mother's memories of a generous, gregarious and kind man. Rosina left little doubt in the minds of all who knew her as to how fond she was of her father and just what a terrible blow his loss had been to her. Her mother was left to bring up her young family alone. She suffered greatly from arthritis in the legs and hips and became very dependent upon her children as they grew up. Rosina's mother ran a small grocery shop on Belgrave Road, which became the central meeting point of the Field brothers and sisters and their children. Rosie, as she was known to the family, visited her mother daily, helping when she could. Don vividly recalls his mother struggling to get to the shop each day, often carrying two large buckets of coal with her in order to stoke the fires when she got there. As young as he was he sensed how difficult caring for his grandmother was but always looked forward to the trips, knowing that one or more of his cousins would be there to play with him. Informal family gatherings of this kind were a welcome relief from the loneliness of his world as an only child.

Charles Maclean worked long and hard hours as a sheet-metal worker on the other side of Birmingham, which required him to leave the house early in the morning and return tired and hungry in the evening. This daily routine stuck vividly in Don's mind. Whilst appreciating that he was one of the more fortunate children of his late war generation, in having a father in a 'reserved' occupation who was not sent away to war, he still saw very little of him during this period of his life. Each morning Charles left the house for work before his son was awake and every evening Don would stand at the front door waiting for his father to appear round the corner at the top of the street. At first glimpse he ran as fast as his legs could carry him until his hand was clasped tightly in his father's. Together they walked proudly and briskly back towards the family home, his father's long strides demanding two or three steps from Don in order to keep up with him. Once inside the house the daily ritual continued as Don watched his father roll up his shirt sleeves and wash himself thoroughly with carbolic soap and cold water at the kitchen sink. The wash was followed by the evening meal and a sleep in the armchair of their living room—the chair belonged to his father and the thought of sitting in it himself never entered Don's mind. Two hours later Charles would stir sufficiently to drink a mug of cocoa, eat two biscuits and climb the stairs to bed.

In a strange way Don gained a lot from these years of observing his father's daily routine. He can recall, even as a very young child, studying the dormant body that sat night after night in the armchair and thinking to himself what an incredible waste of time sleep could become. As a result Don grew up determined to not to spend more time asleep than was absolutely necessary. In contrast to his father he developed an energetic and lively outlook on life.

Weekends in Ombersley Road were a strange mixture of pain and joy. The pain came in Charles Maclean's insistence that his son should eat meat. It was a well-meant discipline but was made more difficult by his mother who happily left Don to enjoy his chosen vegetarian diet during the week. On Sunday mornings the boy was forced to eat the bacon prepared especially for that day's breakfast. Far from finding this the treat it was intended to be Don recalls chewing for what seemed like hours, finding himself unable to swallow, until the end result was a lump of white elastic-like substance left sticking to his teeth. His large ginger tomcat, Tiddles, frequently came to the rescue. As a very young child Don had been given the kitten and they developed a close and affectionate relationship, playing together for hours during the evenings. On Sunday mornings Tiddles would sit quietly at Don's side, patiently waiting to relieve the child of his least favourite breakfast. Don knew that if he could get his hand to his mouth and then down to the cat without his father seeing, the cat would dutifully oblige by eating the meat for him. The task wasn't an easy one as his father sat at the table with him but over the years he success-fully perfected the art. What amazed Don more than anything was the way in which Tiddles sensed that he couldn't let Don down by being seen chewing the bacon. Consequently the cat never put the food on the floor as he would have done in normal circumstances and always managed to stop chewing himself whenever Don's father would look down at him. Don is eternally grateful to Tiddles but the unpleasant experience was sufficiently strong to cause him never willingly to eat meat again.

The much brighter and more enjoyable parts of family weekends came on Sunday afternoons. One luxury in the Maclean household was the possession of a car. Because of this and the fact that the family took regular holidays at the seaside, many of the neighbours thought them wealthy and a little set apart from others living in the Sparkbrook community. However Don was in no doubt as to the advantages of owning a car—regular trips out to local beauty spots provided a pleasure that succeeded in outbalancing the Sunday morning endurance of being made to eat bacon.

In contrast to his father with his strict and steady routine, Don's mother lived life at whirlwind speed. As a child he felt sure that her pace came close to reaching 100mph! Rosie was an intelligent, capable woman whose life was geared to the needs of her husband, son and mother. Don was undoubtedly her pride and joy and it was through her love of playing the piano that he first learned to sing and perform at a very early age. Old-time music-hall songs, popular songs of the day and Catholic hymns were among the wide repertoire that he built as a very young child. Remembering words and lines never appeared a problem to the small boy who later, on entering school, found singing lessons tiresome, boring and without any challenge.

As he grew older Don began to realize that his mother often held rather strange attitudes towards other people. She wasn't a great socializer and remained convinced that few people actually liked her as a person. Don always found it rather puzzling how she arrived at such conclusions without any real evidence or experience of the individuals concerned but he found that he was in danger of developing similar opinions. It was only when he entered his teenage years that he began to recognize her slight tendency towards paranoia. The effects of this experience with his mother had a very positive impact upon him. He decided very early on that he would assume that people liked him unless they clearly showed him otherwise. In hindsight, as a performer, he now realizes how important this has been in developing relationships with audiences. To have gone on stage believing that you were disliked would have been disastrous.

In between caring for her family, Rosie Maclean carefully slotted into the hours that remained various jobs, from domestic cleaning to shop work, in order to supplement the family income. All this helped provide the luxury of a family car and the all-important annual visits to holiday camps. She was hard-working, kind and sincere and a devout Roman

Catholic. Her faith was undoubtedly one of the most important things in her life and something she was determined to pass on to her only son.

Don learned early on in his life that he was unlikely to have younger brothers or sisters. His mother had endured a long and difficult labour prior to his own birth, that had given his father cause for great consternation and a resolve never to allow his wife to go through the experience again. Consequently the energies of both parents were focused on their one child and their expectations were set high. Charles Maclean had been denied the chance of a good education and was determined that his son would take full advantage of the opportunities he was given. The privilege and value of learning were impressed upon Don from an early age. He clearly remembers his father saying, 'No son of mine will get his hands dirty.' Whilst still at primary school he realized that his confidence and ability in reading and writing were something that his father, in particular, did not share. Some years later, on his twenty-first birthday, Don received an envelope containing a gift of money. Written on the front by his father were the words, 'Happy Birthday Mate'. He kept the envelope for years, knowing just how much time and effort the writing of those few words would have taken. It meant a great deal to Don.

The handling of official documents in the Maclean household—the reading and filling out of post-war ration forms and the sorting of bills—quickly became his responsibility. They received very few letters but all the official window-type envelopes that came through the door were immediately handed to Don. From the age of just seven or eight not only did he read them but he was often left to make the decisions as to how they were to be dealt with. Not appreciating that such tasks were any different to those expected of other children of his age, he carried them out without question. On reflection Don realizes that there were times during his childhood when he both felt and took the adult role in the home. But those feelings never outweighed the fact that he knew he was loved, secure and supported by his parents throughout both his childhood and the succeeding years. If anything, the knowledge that they did everything to ensure that he achieved his potential in so many different ways fills Don with deep gratitude and respect for them.

Life at home for this only child was often quiet and very lonely, especially during long, dark winter evenings when he was unable to play on the street with other children. Don spent many hours creating imaginary friends and games. His vivid imagination enabled him to fight and win battles, football games, table tennis and numerous other sporting adventures all within the confines of his head and the living room.

Family parties were among the more memorable times of real entertainment with others. The great number of aunts, uncles and cousins on Don's mother's side of the family would crowd into each other's homes several times a year. Without the instant modern-day entertainment of television and videos the family spent many hours creating their own amusement. Everyone took part each offering their contribution towards an impromptu concert. Don's regular turn would be to stand alongside his mother at the piano and sing his well-rehearsed songs.

One cousin in particular remembers Don as a rather quiet and sensitive child, often needing his mother's encouragement to sing at family parties in his younger days. Pat spent a lot of time in her Aunt Rosie and Uncle Charlie's home having lost her own mother when she was seven years of age. Trips to the park and cinema were shared with them as a family and the two cousins enjoyed a close friendship even though there was a five-year age difference between them. She has never forgotten one particular visit to the cinema to watch the film *Bambi*—an occasion which confirms her memory of Don as a sensitive and caring child. The moving story of the orphaned deer is well known and loved by millions of children but he proved to be moved more than most. Don was so upset at the killing of Bambi's mother that he cried loudly until Pat had to take him home, in order to console him and leave others to watch the film in peace. Years later Don gave Pat a copy of the video *Bambi* with the message: 'Now you can watch the end in peace and quiet.'

Despite his cautious beginnings Don's confidence did grow with age and it wasn't long before he was expanding his act at family parties to include a whole string of jokes that he had either made up himself or heard on the radio. There is no doubt in his mind that the seeds of comedy and entertainment in him were sown through radio. Voluntarily going to bed on a Sunday afternoon in order to be allowed to stay up to listen to 'Variety Bandbox' during the evening was, in his mind, a very small price to pay in return for the enjoyment received. The variety show consisted of a series of acts linked by BBC compère Philip Slessor and was designed to present to the public the more 'with it' singers and comedians of the day. It became the show in which the stars of the future emerged. Amongst them were artists such as Derek Roy, Arthur English, Peter Sellers, Bill Kerr and the brilliant Frankie Howerd, who rocketed to fame through 'Variety Bandbox'. It was here that thousands of listeners heard for the first time his devastating catchphrases such as 'chilly', 'just get myself comfy' 'what a funny woman' and 'I was amazed'. It was a comic style unlike anything ever heard on the air up until that time and one that shaped and channelled the humour of this small boy in ways that were to grow far beyond the expectations of either his parents or himself. Not only did he enjoy repeating the patter of the comedians but their humour obviously stimulated and sharpened his own powers of observation. Even at this young age Don began to study people and their reactions, looking always for the funny side of things, and quickly developed a real love of the ridiculous.

Family holidays at Warner camps provided him with further opportunities to test out his talent upon largely supportive audiences of parents and children. Ambitious and enthusiastic children lined up in the wings ready to take the stage. Some sang, others danced and a few of the brave and foolish would tell their string of jokes. Don looked forward each year to the competitions, carefully preparing his act, and his efforts were not in vain. He started with character impressions, occasionally slipping in a gag or two, and generally finishing off with a song. He quickly learned that if he selected a current pop single the teenage contingent of the audience would applaud loudly in support of the song, regardless of the voice quality of the singer. Judges never failed to respond to the reaction of an audience, consequently there was never a holiday from which he didn't bring home a much treasured award or prize from the talent shows. Such experiences became the foundation stone on which the Don Maclean act of many years later was built.

During the latter years at Clifton Road Primary School, at the ages of ten and eleven, Don went out of his way to find an audience—and particularly one that laughed. As an 'A' stream pupil in a class of forty-three children his attempts at achieving a laugh were not always appreciated by class teacher Mrs Philips. She was quick to recognize Don's quick-thinking ability in the academic world as well as that of comedy, and knew full well the high expectations of his parents for him to succeed at school. It was her responsibility to prepare him for the eleven-plus examination and ensure him a place at grammar school but it took some months to convince the aspiring comedian of his need to work hard.

The first of six terms together was a battle of wills between Don and his teacher. It was the first time anyone had made him work. During the first four years at school everything had come easily to him—meeting the required standards had demanded little effort or concentration from this bright child. Gradually, the two achieved a greater understanding of each other and life became easier for both. Don particularly enjoyed Mrs Philips' tales of her husband's time in the Royal Air Force, and was impressed by her own knowledge of the war and particularly aircraft. He left no one in any doubt as to his ambition in life. 'I'm going to be a pilot,' he announced to the class with an air of confidence and determination that firmly convinced his teacher that one day his dream would become a reality.

At times he was considered a positive thorn in the side, making his presence felt in more than one way. Singing lessons were his pet hate—and Mrs Philips' only opportunity to hand her large class over to another teacher for just one lesson a week. Don was regularly sent to stand in the passageway outside her room as punishment for having expressed his forthright opinion on the choice of songs and music. Much to his class teacher's relief, the headmistress intervened and escorted the strongly-opinionated child to her office where he happily spent future singing lessons working towards his eleven-plus examination. It proved to be time well spent.

With his endless questions and very inquisitive mind Don made a lasting impression on Mrs Philips. She could not deny his high intelligence and what she often thought an unusually adult outlook on life for a child of his age. They enjoyed lengthy conversations on a wide range of different topics over their two years together. Don remembers her as one of the few school teachers who treated him as an equal whilst at the same time managing to bring out the best in him at an academic level. Not only did he succeed in passing the eleven-plus examination but his marks fell within the top 2 per cent of all children in the Birmingham education authority for that year. He felt a tremendous sense of achievement and the success gave his parents a great deal of joy and pride.

Don's roots were firmly planted both in Sparkbrook and in the security of a caring home and family. It was an environment that clearly contained all the necessary ingredients for the healthy growth and development of a young boy. But there was one component that Don found particularly engaging. It had been there from the very beginning, deepening and enriching every aspect of his life. This influence of the Christian faith in Don's life—through the Roman Catholic Church—was fanned into life by his mother but the responsibility for its growth and nurture in his childhood years was shared by two other very special women. Their influence was to extend way beyond his childhood years and indeed beyond their own lifespans.

2

God and Three Women

The decision to have Don baptized into the Roman Catholic faith was never the subject of debate or discussion. His mother's convictions were strong and deeply rooted in her own childhood, and she had every intention of passing this faith onto her only son. In contrast Charles Maclean showed no particular religious leanings and had very little time for the institution of the church. As a boy he had sung in a Church of England choir but admitted to being more attracted by the money that the choir boys earned than by appreciation of the music or worship. It wasn't long before regular church attendance ceased to be part of his childhood years and so he continued into his adult life. However, he never allowed his own thoughts and feelings to influence the decision about Don's spiritual upbringing. His only son was to be baptized and nurtured in the Christian faith, within the structures of the Roman Catholic Church. Whilst he did not play an active part in that process, he was fully supportive of the decision made for Don as a young baby. Important landmarks in Don's spiritual journey, such as his baptism, first Holy Communion and confirmation, were always shared by his father and Don remains confident that whilst his father never showed any desire or need to be part of a worshipping community, he did hold a quiet and confident faith in God.

Don's baptism at the church of St John the Evangelist, Balsall Heath, outwardly marked the beginning of a lifelong journey of faith, the early stages of which were clearly influenced by his mother. Each morning after his father had gone to work she would kneel by the bedside in her room to say her prayers. Don would often stand at the door and watch the peaceful and serene look on his mother's face as she spoke to the God in whom she trusted. Regularly at bedtime she would teach Don to do the same, as together they knelt to pray. This nightly communion with God not only provided a structure to his life that would remain with him throughout his childhood and into adulthood but also served to strengthen the bonds between mother and son.

Regular attendance at the 9a.m. mass on a Sunday morning became an important part of his weekly routine. As early as two and three years of age he recalls standing with his mother in a pew near to the back of a full church packed with between two and three hundred worshippers each week. Frequently people would stand, crowding out the aisles, when there were too few seats to accommodate them all. The atmosphere was electric to the small boy. He studied his mother's concentration in worship and stillness in prayer and envied the way in which she always appeared so tranquil and at one with God. In contrast he struggled to maintain concentration at those quietest moments, always wanting to look around in order to see, hear and know exactly what was going on in the service. The Latin mass, as it was then, fed the dramatic and theatrical spirit of this young child; colour, movement, sounds and symbolism captured his vivid imagination. At home he had been introduced to the mass through an illustrated children's book explaining for each stage of the service exactly what the priest was doing and why. Don and his mother spent many hours at bedtime reading and rereading the book until it became so familiar Don could recite parts of the liturgy and explanation by heart.

Much of the service's deeper theological meaning went way beyond the limits of his young mind, as did the Latin but his spirit and emotions were richly nourished. It was a spiritual experience that he could always feel inside, extending way beyond the limitations of the body, mind and understanding.

The physical surroundings of the church building and its contents helped. There was always something to look at, absorbing the interest and curiosity of a small child: the deep rich colours worn by the priest that changed with the seasons of the church year, the smell of incense infiltrating the atmosphere, the lighted candles, the enormous crucifix hanging above the altar and the sound of bells announcing important and significant parts of the service. As the priest approached the tabernacle (where consecrated bread is reserved) and all heads were bowed, Don recalls being desperate to peep to see what was happening but knew that he would not move until the bell had sounded. All his senses were stimulated through the cere-mony, enriching his total experience of worship. He particularly loved looking at the statues of Jesus and the saints. Every one had its own identity and meaning and he would stare intently at each. He noticed with a sense of wonder and fascination that whenever he looked at the statue of Mary, mother of Jesus, she always appeared to be looking directly at him. Even when he changed places or shifted positions, the loving eyes and a tender spirit that he had so often seen and recognized in his own mother were looking down upon him. The whole atmosphere was warm and comforting, never frightening or distanced.

This was Don's church; he was part of the family of that worshipping community. Dozens of children crowded into the congregation each week, many of whom attended the primary school linked with St John's. It was Don's dream to be allowed to sit with these children, who gathered as a large group in the pews situated to the right of the side aisle of the church. One Sunday, long before he was of school age or able to read and follow any service book, he decided for himself that it was time to join this group of older children. Picking up a book at the end of the pew, Don stood straight, proud to be able to identify with the children of the church. He was unable to read or understand what was going on but simply standing there imitating the actions of the older ones was sufficient for him to feel included and part of that body. He can only have been three or four years of age but the memory of this moment remains clear in his mind.

Clifton Road Primary School was not Rosie Maclean's first choice of school for her five-year-old son. She had never dreamt of him attending anything other than a Roman Catholic school, where she could be sure that he would receive clear teaching about the basics of the faith he had been baptized into as a young baby. In her mind, religious education was much more than the one or two academic lessons timetabled at some point in the week as so many viewed it. It was more about learning a way of being which embraces the whole of life: work, rest and play. Rosie knew from first-hand experience that a Roman Catholic school would provide not only religious instruction but also opportunity for worship and friendship with like-minded children all through the week. It would also reinforce the values and standards that she sought to pass onto Don in the home. It was everything she had always wanted for her son.

It came as a great disappointment to her, therefore, when she failed to get a place for her son at the nearest Roman Catholic primary school. The family lived close to the boundary of two Roman Catholic parishes, both of which disputed their eligibility on the grounds of where they lived. Each one claimed that the Macleans lived within the catchment area for the other school. The confusion went on for some months until finally there were no places left at either school, by which time Don was five and a half years old and well past the legal age for starting school. The end result was that he was sent, albeit reluctantly on his mother's part, to the local non-Catholic primary school, along with many of the children living around about. Don spent six very happy years there and the lack of a Roman Catholic influence in his education at this stage strengthened his identity as a Roman Catholic, rather than weakening it as his mother had feared.

He discovered that he was the only Roman Catholic in the school and became very proud of it, developing quite a missionary spirit. Teachers often went out of their way to make him feel special rather than different, taking time to explain how celebration, prayer and worship at festival times might differ slightly for Don from that of his classmates. Don would deliberately make a point of his faith, always saying the shorter, Roman Catholic version of the Lord's Prayer louder and more clearly than others and making sure that his 'Amen' was a solo, timed at least a line or two before his classmates had finished praying. On occasions he managed to say a quick 'Hail Mary' prayer before they had reached 'Amen'. He remembers a time when he became very moral and even prudish, sensing the responsibility that he had in representing both his faith and his church in a Protestant environment. On reflection Don recognizes the importance of these formative years; he was given an opportunity to express his faith and felt very affirmed as a young Roman Catholic by non-Catholics. Strong and healthy development was taking place in the whole child—body, mind and spirit—contrary to what his mother had feared in placing him at the Clifton Road school.

Rosina Maclean didn't leave anything to chance. Even though Don had shown that he was happy at primary school, showing no signs of spiritual decline or disadvantage, she still had a conscience about him not receiving what she understood as 'proper' instruction in his faith. Most children baptized as Roman Catholics would expect to be prepared for and take their first Holy Communion by the time they were seven or eight years of age. Don reached the age of seven and had not received any instruction other than his weekly attendance at mass. It played on his mother's mind until she took the matter into her own hands and approached a lady whom she knew to be a teacher at one of the Roman Catholic primary schools that Don had failed to get into.

Monday to Friday Miss Freda King had responsibility for the reception class at the school and was a regular worshiper at the 9a.m. Sunday mass at St John's Church, Balsall Heath. The memory of Don's mother approaching her outside church one Sunday morning remains clear in her mind. She remembers her as a troubled woman in need of offloading a great burden of guilt and anxiety. Rosina felt sure that she was failing in her duty as a mother by not sending her son to a Catholic school and was desperate for him to somehow receive instruction from the Church outside school hours. Unbeknown to her, several other children were in identical situations and were already meeting on a Saturday morning at the local convent school for their catechism classes. Miss King arranged for Don and his mother to meet the Reverend Mother of the convent in order that Don could join the class. Rosina was relieved, delighted and grateful to Miss King for her help.

Their delight was doubled the following Saturday morning when Don was introduced to his new catechism teacher—Miss Freda King. Many children would dread the thought of two hours' additional learning on a Saturday morning but not Don. He was a lively seven year old with an unusually large appetite for learning Catholic catechism. His missionary spirit revealed itself once more as he encouraged others to join him at the classes. For every new child that was brought along, a holy picture—of Jesus or one of the saints— would be presented to the inviter. As time went on Don's bedroom became a gallery of holy pictures. Some of the children in his new class were younger than he, so he assumed a parent role, quickly learning everything he was taught so that he might help teach the others in the group. The other children sat in awe of the speed at which he acquired this knowledge. Don absorbed everything he was taught like a sponge. And Miss King's warmth and personality made the learning so much more enjoyable than many of his midweek lessons. She was always full of fun and laughter, with an enormous amount of enthusiasm for all that she was teaching. It was a combination that worked well for them both. There were times when Miss King felt Don was a child 'set apart' from the others, with a faith and hunger for spiritual things that she had rarely encountered before. It was her joy and privilege to feed this hunger.

A very special relationship developed between Don and his teachers at the convent during those years. Miss King prepared him both for his First Communion and Confirmation whilst a nun called Sister Annuncia taught him in between times. The two women merge into one in his memory as an adult and he finds it hard to distinguish between two of the most Christian people he ever knew.

Sister Annuncia appeared very tall to the young boy, with a habit that enveloped her whole body. From within that black shapeless form she could produce anything, or so it seemed to a child's imagination. Books, pencils, handkerchiefs—even light refreshments on occasions—would emerge just as they were required. He loved to listen to her soft Irish accent which he always thought was like melted butter rolling down the back of his neck, not least when she referred to him as her 'little disciple'. He hung on her every word. She was a well-educated woman, who had studied at Reading University and was a fount of knowledge as far as Don was concerned. One word, or even one look, from Sister Annuncia was sufficient not only to silence Don but call him to immediate attention. He'd have done anything to please this sincere and devout woman. On particularly bad days at home when he had been misbehaving, his mother would threaten to tell the Sister of his misdemeanours. It always had an immediate effect. To cause either of these women any grief through bad behaviour would have filled Don with a shame and embarrassment he felt sure he'd never get over.

Don Maclean and Napoleon Bonaparte have at least one important thing in common: both have held the occasion of their first Holy Communion as one of the greatest days of their lives. Don was the first of his catechism class to be put forward.

Miss King and Sister Annuncia had prepared him well and were extremely proud of their eager young disciple. The Reverend Mother was also to be present, ready to play her all-important role in the service. She was as small as Sister Annuncia was tall and had an equally enchanting accent but this time it was French. Beautiful terms of endearment would fall from her lips, causing Don to melt in her presence. *Mon brave* or *Mon enfant* were not translated by his knowledge of another language but interpreted within the context of the love and affection with which they were spoken.

Miss King, Sister Annuncia and the Reverend Mother stood waiting for Don to arrive early for the 9a.m. mass. Wearing short trousers, jacket, shirt and tie and with his hair firmly stuck to his head with brylcreem he stood perfectly still as Sister Annuncia pinned a dark red sash over his shoulder. Along with his parents and teachers he took up his reserved position at the front of the church. Every Sunday he watched the Reverend Mother take her Holy Communion first but on this occasion that was to be his privilege. She moved out of the pew to allow Don to come to the front. '*Après toi*—after you,' she whispered gently encouraging him towards the altar where the priest was waiting to receive him. At that moment of his first Holy Communion, he knew that he had become a fully participating member of the church community, joining the many other children and adults with whom he had worshipped since he had been baptized. And he had drawn closer to God himself. After the service, grown men and women stood waiting to shake his hand, as a sign of the welcome they offered one more growing member of their church family. It was an experience that he was never to forget.

Miss King wanted to mark the occasion with a personal gift. Taking Don to the stall at the back of church she told him to chose something that he would really like. He selected a statue of Mary, the mother of Jesus, similar to the one he had spent so many years studying in the services. It cost two shillings and sixpence but to Don it was priceless. He kept it in his bedroom as a reminder of his special day. The following week, back in his Saturday morning class, several of the children had tired of the attention bestowed upon Don for this occasion. They teased him unkindly by saying that they would be having their first Holy Communions in a group and would be having a big party after the service. He was totally unaffected by their teasing and simply reminded them that partying had little to do with the real meaning of receiving this sign of God's presence. Once more Miss King stood back amazed at the way in which this young child had so obviously experienced the reality of faith in God.

There was just one part of his early Christian instruction that came not from his Saturday morning class but from a Protestant nonconformist chapel near to his home in Sparkbrook. The small missionary-style church often ran groups for local children after school or during the early evening on week-days. Dozens of children would gather to learn songs and choruses and hear a different story from the Bible each week. The focus of this time was clearly Bible learning. He loved every minute of his time spent there, eager to hear as much as he could but soon learned of his mother's disapproval. Having never experienced anything other than a Catholic influence on her faith, Rosie Maclean was very unhappy about her son receiving instruction from another church. She feared that it might conflict with Roman Catholic teaching and so discouraged Don from attending. On occasions he ran the risk of disobeying her, in order to learn more and more about the treasures of this book. Now, as an adult, he is saddened by what he feels is an inadequate knowledge of the Bible and wishes that he had received more opportunity for learning about it as a child.

Don cannot recall a time in his life when he has not believed in God. Through the influence of his mother, God was there in the very beginning. His faith was a natural and fully integrated part of his upbringing. Very early on in his catechism class he was taught that everyone has a guardian angel—a messenger from God. Miss King described the angel as a light that lived on the shoulders. That image was helpful and comforting for Don, enabling him to believe that God was not restricted to any one time or place but was always with him wherever he went and whatever he was doing. The relationship was also clearly a two-way one. There was never any sense in which God was the only giver and Don the only taker. From when he was a small boy, he knew that part of that relationship involved Don serving God, not simply God serving Don.

His childhood images of God were often those which he had seen in stained-glass windows, statues or picture books—an old man with a long white beard who was to be feared, especially if Don had done something wrong. At times he worried that God would exact vengeance on him for his wrongdoing but this anxiety never stopped him from approaching God. Don knew that in admitting his wrongdoing he would find God's forgiveness and always found the Roman Catholic practice of confessing sins to a priest helpful. He also felt that the loving and comforting figure of Mary, mother of Jesus and, later, that of Jesus himself, helped bring him closer to God.

Three completely different women laid the spiritual foundations in Don Maclean's life. Each brought their own invaluable contribution: a mother whose love and devotion created opportunities for learning and pointed her son in the right direction; a teacher whose instruction, laughter and wisdom fed his eager and hungry spirit and a nun whose humanity and spirituality blended to provide an infectious attraction towards a depth of faith which grew as he developed. Don acquired his faith not by academic learning but through experiencing God in and through both the lives of these three women and Holy Communion. That experience has lived with him throughout his life and his relationship with God continues to thrive and grow.

3

St Philip's Grammar School

Don was one of the first in his class to receive his highly successful eleven-plus examination result and to be told that he had been allocated a place at the senior school of his first choice, St Philip's Roman Catholic Grammar School, in Edgbaston. Two days later, due to his exceptionally good results he was also offered a much-coveted scholarship place at Birmingham's King Edward's High School. In his mother's mind there was no choice. She had finally succeeded in obtaining the Roman Catholic education for her son that she had always longed for. Along with twenty-eight other Catholic boys drawn from all over the city Don was admitted into a specially graded 'z' form for outstanding achievers of that year's entry into the school. These boys were expected to take their 'O' level examinations in four years instead of the usual five and to study more subjects than the other two forms in their year. This privileged treatment boosted Don's confidence even more and created a strong bonding between the boys in the class.

St Philip's held a fine reputation for providing both a high standard of academic teaching and also sound physical, moral and religious training. Boys came from widely diverse backgrounds and travelled from all over Birmingham. It also had strong links with both the Roman Catholic Oratory church (run by the Oratorian religious order) and St Paul's Roman Catholic school for girls. When the school was founded in 1887, the then Bishop of Birmingham, William Bernard, gave it his full blessing, stating in a letter:

> *It gives me great satisfaction to know that the Oratorian fathers are contemplating a Grammar School for Birmingham. It is a want that has been felt for some time past, and I trust the undertaking will receive due support from the laity, both in encouraging the School and in providing it with pupils. When a good secular can be combined with a good religious education it argues great neglect of duty when parents abandon this advantage for their sons.*

Rosie Maclean was finally satisfied that she was no longer neglecting her duty in providing the best of religious and secular education for her son. That essential religious element was now integrated into the whole of his learning. Even though the journey from Sparkbrook to Edgbaston took some thirty minutes, making the day considerably longer than Don had experienced at Clifton Road Primary, he rose to the challenge. It was to develop and stretch him academically, socially, spiritually and physically.

Don struck up friendships within minutes of arriving on that first day, some of which he was to keep not only throughout the five years at St Philip's but for many years following. He and Pat Barr clicked together immediately and shared a strong interest in both amateur dramatics and the football field, where together they created hours of entertainment and mischief. Eddie Butler and Don were also drawn together, particularly by their similar working-class backgrounds—not least by the discovery early on that their mothers had been educated together some forty years earlier.

Both friends recall with clarity their first meeting with Don. He displayed a confidence beyond his eleven years of age, with a personality that emerged in all aspects of school life. Even the religious side of their education did not escape his rapidly developing humour. The close connection with the Birmingham Oratory meant that it was not unusual for boys to attend confession or mass in the lunch hour, when girls from St Paul's were also often in attendance. Within a few weeks Don had worked out the different Oratorians' individual idiosyncrasies and foibles, especially in connection with confessions. It was fertile ground for schoolboy humour, particularly where one profoundly deaf priest was concerned. He compensated for his inability to hear by fearing the very worst about a boy's confession and issuing somewhat severe penances. It became customary amongst the boys to compare their 'punishments' in such circumstances and Don frequently revelled in the speculation of another's sins. His quick quips and humour provided many a moment's entertainment amidst the more serious religious side of school life.

Whilst academically quite able, he was to excel first and foremost on the sports field. There had been few opportunities for taking sport seriously in the primary school; the emphasis of the annual sports day had been more on a spirit of participation than strong competition and had done little to satisfy the fierce competitive streak in the eleven-year-old boy. Now he found the opportunity not only to compete at a much higher standard but to enter into a wide range of sporting disciplines. Football remained his first passion; although not always the most skilled, Don compensated with speed, power and enthusiasm, rarely failing to earn himself a place in the school team. He became a valued team member, not least because his strong personality and ability to create laughter united the boys in a way that often benefited their game.

The Colts XI (under-fifteens) were a particularly successful year team, inspired by the English master known as 'The Masher' (because of his frequently used catchphrase, 'I'll mash you, boy!'). His frequent praise of Don as a keen and spirited player was to be heard in an equally familiar expression which announced, 'Maclean, you gotta spark!' No one was ever quite sure what was meant by many of Masher's somewhat unusual expressions for a Doctor of Literature—but one thing was sure, the boys never failed to respond to his every word. Whilst it may not have been hero worship, it was definitely some kind of worship; they believed The Masher was the greatest master they would ever know. On one occasion he produced some football socks which were more hole than sock, asking, 'Would anyone's kind mother be willing to darn...?' Rosie Maclean was the 'kind mother' on that occasion although The Masher didn't hold the same affection for fathers who turned up to watch their sons play. Convinced that they were nothing but a distraction, he did all within his powers to dissuade them from attending important matches. Don's father was one of the brave who chose to ignore the advice and rarely missed one of his son's games. That year they completed the hat trick: champions of the league, Grammar Schools' Cup and Catholic Cup. Don's memories of that period and the obvious affection that all the boys had for the rather eccentric master were demonstrated years later when they became the inspiration for a local newspaper sports feature article entitled 'The Masher's Finest Hour!' The colourful description of the Catholic Cup final in the presence of the Archbishop and numerous other priests and nuns, not to mention Don's own rather painful injury, made humorous and entertaining reading.

Throughout his five years at St Philip's, Don represented the school in every sport except for cricket. Whilst football was his main passion, athletics became his most successful discipline. In trying a variety of distances he both sprinted and battled his way through mud and wet on cross-country tracks but finally settled for the middle distance of 800 metres. Success whilst representing the school led to county trials and a place on the Warwickshire county team. Don's father revelled in his son's success, never missing the opportunity to stand on the track-side cheering him on.

St Philip's prided themselves on high standards in most sports but swimming was undoubtedly an area in which they excelled. Situated close by a good competitive-size swimming pool, they had access to the best facilities. The boys were some of the few schoolchildren of their day privileged to receive swimming instruction as part of their weekly sports curriculum and it was here that Don developed both a love of the water and a strong competitive stroke. There was hardly a school year when he didn't represent the school both in individual and relay races. Lifesaving was another aspect of swimming that was taken very seriously. For many years the school had a class that was affiliated to the Royal Life-Saving Society, providing boys with the opportunity to take their bronze medallion or intermediate certificate award. Classes took place on Wednesday afternoons and Don signed up at the first opportunity, never realizing at the time just what an asset his life-saving certificate would be in the future in starting him off on the road to show business.

St Philip's also had a strong tradition of amateur dramatics, the highlight of which became the annual school play, usually a Shakespearean production. Each year auditions were held, along with the girls from the nearby St Paul's school—which in itself provided great incentive for the boys to attend. Don and his friends were often first to sign up for audition and managed to secure themselves roles in three consecutive years' productions including *As You Like It*, *Julius Caesar* and *Macbeth*. School friend Pat Barr recalls a memorable performance of Don as Macduff in *Macbeth* but it was the duo's practical joking that surfaced most prominently in his memory of those plays. Their form had a particularly bad reputation for playing pranks on unsuspecting boys, masters or priests but on the opening night of *As You Like It* they chose to expose the fruit of their antics to the whole audience. A group of boys had practised playing their recorders for some weeks, in order to give background accompaniment to the opening scene, including the well-known line, 'If music be the food of love, play on.' On this occasion Don and Pat stuffed the recorder ends with chalk just before the performance was due to start. The result was a muffled noise barely resembling music, least of all a love song. The boys faces grew redder and redder in their feeble attempts to produce an acceptable sound. Other years' antics never quite achieved the same impact or degree of success but the boys were rarely short of ideas or courage in their attempts to bring laughter and chaos into the more serious and studious aspects of school life.

Don was never slow to participate in pranks initiated by other members of his form and there was always a strong solidarity when it came to owning up. One particular science master at St Philip's regularly became the butt of jokes and no more so than on the day he was locked into the chemical store cupboard by a certain member of Don's form. The culprit was well known to the whole class but not one of them was willing to reveal his identity. Their closing of ranks was tested to the full when the entire form received a full term's detention as punishment. Don happily stood by his peers on such occasions, with a secret regard for their accomplishments. His admiration extended even further towards those who performed the most successful of pranks with no recognition from their peers at all. One such occasion was when sixteen or more of the boys' toilets were locked from the inside, leaving hundreds of desperate pupils feeling somewhat uncomfortable. It was several hours before anyone realized that the lavatories were unoccupied and no one ever admitted responsibility. Don felt sure that if it had been him, he would have basked in the glory and limelight of success—something he realized that he was learning to enjoy even at this age.

Whilst performing Shakespeare in school, Don still found other opportunities for performance of a very different kind outside school. His parents continued to take him to holiday camps each summer where he revelled in the success of children's talent shows but one particular year such opportunities came a little closer to home. The Birmingham Parks department held 'Search for a Star' competitions in the city's major parks. Large tents were erected and posters were displayed encouraging children and young people to enter the talent shows. Don didn't need to be told twice. He practised his singing and impressions of Jerry Lewis, Ted Lune, Terry Scott and even Kathleen Ferrier, ready for the performance. He was doubly motivated by the fact that the prize on this occasion was money. First prize in the heats was half a crown of saving stamps but if you got through to the final it was a full ten shillings. The grand final of finals of all the parks was heralded as a platform for up-and-coming stars. Don soon learned that he could enter for more than one park competition, even if they were on the same day. By travelling around Birmingham on his bicycle from park to park he soon earned himself a considerable quantity of saving stamps as well as a couple of ten-shilling notes. It felt good to be rewarded with money, not because he was particularly mercenary but because it made him feel that his performance had been worth something. He recalls his father proudly telling him, 'If they pay you, lad, you know that you are good.' It was affirmation of this kind that encouraged Don as he developed his stage act.

Success in the parks boosted his confidence and widened his reputation in the low-key world of amateur entertainment. He soon found himself working with a small group of people who would take concert parties around the local hospitals, the old people's homes and occasionally the prisons. The audiences were all very supportive and appreciative of his time and talent. Once more he was rewarded financially, this time with travel expenses, which nearly always exceeded the costs he had incurred. Don couldn't believe that he was being paid to do what he loved most. Hobbies usually cost money to do—but his was paying him to enjoy it. It provided the incentive to work hard at his performances, always on the look-out for new jokes and material, much of which came from the hours he spent listening to the radio.

The medium of radio continued to be the greatest influence upon Don during these years at St Philip's. Whenever possible he went to the cinema to watch Jerry Lewis and Dean Martin films and sometimes got to see a live show in Birmingham. Occasionally he managed to persuade his parents to take him to the Hippodrome, where he saw Archie Andrews and Roy Rogers but the majority of his leisure time was spent listening to the radio at home. Televisions were still a luxury owned by a minority but families regularly gathered together for many hours of happy listening.

Comedy-type programmes produced by the BBC's Variety department had played an important role during the war years in providing light relief amidst the pressures surrounding families separated by thousands of miles and others bereaved of loved ones. The task of bringing a little joy amidst the sorrow was a challenge taken very seriously by war-time producers and continued during these early post-war years. The archives of radio history clearly recognize that Michael Standing did more than anyone to improve the standards of light entertainment at this time and several legendary programmes and performers emerged from his time as director of 'Variety'. Gradually the morale of the nation was raised and tensions relaxed, all of which had its effects upon broadcasting. Radio comedy generally became less elitist and more in tune with ordinary people. In contrast to the thirties and forties, programmes became a lot more outspoken, jokes were broader and the humour once restricted to the barrackroom became more and more commonplace on the air. However the general guidelines and standards enforced by the BBC's famous Green Book ensured that programmes entertained without 'giving reasonable offence to any part of its diversified audience... free from vulgarity, political bias, and matter in questionable taste.' A new wave of entertainers, many ex-servicemen who had served the British troops in wartime shows, were slowly emerging from serving in North Africa and Iceland, or even the skies over Germany. They were the people and programmes that shaped and channelled the humour of this youthful budding entertainer, who soaked up all the comedy resources that he could.

Among the legendary programmes was 'The Goon Show'. The original line-up of Peter Sellers, Spike Milligan, Harry Secombe and Michael Bentine first emerged in May 1951 and the show became the longest running comedy programme of its time. It succeeded in echoing the mood of disenchantment that was then current but managed at the same time temporarily to turn the real world on its head. Its absurdity appealed to a thinking audience, who could not afford to lose concentration in case they missed something of this high-speed presentation. It captured the imagination in a fresh and addictive way. Millions became compulsive Goon listeners and Don was one. He and his St Philip's schoolmates never missed a show, its contents becoming the sole topic of conversation throughout the following day. The Goons' humour affected a whole generation of young people and helped to evolve a whole new generation of comedians. Many a leading comedy entertainer of today acknowledges the impact of the Goons on their formative years of humour development.

Other memorable programmes of this period for Don include comedy classics such as 'Take it From Here', featuring Jimmy Edwards, Dick Bentley and Joy Nichols, which after a slow start eventually ran to 325 programmes. It didn't enjoy the high profile of some others, such as Ted Ray's 'Ray's a Laugh' but made a rich contribution to the enormous variety on air at this time. Ted Ray himself was undoubtedly one of the country's leading music-hall comedians during this period, appearing frequently at the London Palladium and as the bill-topper all over Britain. Don could not hear enough of him. He possessed a style that was machine-gun fast with a phenomenal ability to ad lib, the characteristics of which were clearly identifiable in young Maclean's act. He was regarded as a most even-tempered craftsman, whose wit offstage equalled his performance on. Only a few years later Don was to see his show live and meet the man behind the performance. One of Britain's best-known character actresses, Patricia Hayes, worked on the show with Ted, establishing herself as a leading performer, along with Peter Sellers, Kitty Bluett, Fred Yule and Kenneth Connor who provided the brilliant supporting cast. Together they combined many elements of variety and comedy.

The range of radio comedy programmes in the fifties was quite extraordinary. Domestic comedies were plentiful and particularly popular amongst families. 'Meet the Huggets', 'Life with The Lyons' and 'The Clitheroe Kid' all went some way towards reflecting the real world, albeit slightly exaggerated, enabling listeners to identify with the behaviour and situations of these fictional families. During the course of a typical Sunday Don may well have listened to 'Ray's a Laugh', 'Life with The Lyons' and finished off with 'Educating Archie', a programme which over the years became a barometer of success as the showcase of the emerging bill-toppers. It made stars of many, amongst them the Birmingham-born Tony Hancock who became one of Don's all-time favourites. The much acclaimed 'Hancock's Half-Hour', first produced in 1954, pushed the boundaries of radio comedy even further. The dream was to produce a show with no jokes or funny voices, just relying on caricature and situation humour. There would be no breaks, guest singers or catchphrases, something that was quite new to comedy radio. One hundred and one episodes of the show went out. Hancock's sudden death through an overdose of drugs in the sixties left the nation, Don amongst them, mourning the loss of a comic genius.

Schoolfriends remember Don's attitude to humour being

quite different to that of his peers. Whilst he always laughed at what other boys found funny, there was a constant fascination within him surrounding the whole subject of humour. He couldn't simply enjoy it: it had to be discussed, debated and analysed. Pat Barr recalls many visits to see Jerry Lewis films with Don and the post-film debriefing session that took place on the way home, until Don had satisfied himself as to exactly what it was that people were laughing at and why. In hindsight Pat can see the emerging pattern of the entertainer whose life's work became making people laugh. The analytical process of learning how started in these teenage years. Towards their latter years together at St Philip's Pat recalls Don's powerful ability to control the company that he found himself in. Whenever he wanted to impress an individual or group of people—perhaps a girl, a teacher or a football team—he had the natural ability to adapt his behaviour in order to gain their attention. And more often than not, he succeeded. In hindsight Pat sees the very early stages of Don's professional approach to his job as a controller of audiences.

Surprisingly, the world of sport, drama, tent competitions and concert parties still allowed Don time to be a normal teenager and enjoy the strong social gatherings of his peers on a Saturday night, experiencing both the pain and the joy of growing up. He was never really tempted to consume even small quantities of alcohol, as he always hated the smell, never mind the taste but he and Pat Barr did decide to experiment with the delights of tobacco one evening. Carefully selecting an evening when his parents were out, Pat invited Don round to sample one of his father's cigars. It was a brave but disastrous attempt at what both boys thought was being a man. Pat's father returned to find the two boys sat in sub-zero temperatures with all windows open, looking distinctly green and feeling most dreadfully sick. Don was never to smoke again and a number of years later was quick to make his stand as a member of an anti-smoking campaigning group.

An interest in girls was inevitably a strong feature of these teenage years. The Roman Catholic churches had an excellent network of youth clubs for their young people in Birmingham and St Philip's was an ideal channel for advertising the free dances held at different churches each Saturday. It seemed that almost everyone in the school would be there. In contrast to many adolescent boys around him he was rarely short of conversation when it came to chatting up the girls and his mixing both in the Oratory and in school stage productions had given him added confidence. Don became one of the few boys who had a long-term relationship with a girl right up until the time he left St Philip's. He and 'Paddy' Jones, as she was known to her friends, joined the network of youth club dances, becoming an established couple amongst their peers and often made tremendous efforts to meet up in the school holidays.

Pat Barr was persuaded to join Don on one such occasion. Paddy had gone to Pontins Holiday Camp on the south coast and persuaded Don to visit her whilst she was there. Having cycled the whole distance the two boys arrived early in the evening whilst the entire camp was in the dining room. This was to their advantage, as they managed to gain entry over a fence, thereby avoiding the security officers on the main gate. Triumphant with the success of gaining entry, they took themselves off to the swimming pool where they discovered two attractive young ladies who were very happy to be entertained by the young men. Foolishly Don disclosed the details of their dishonest access, only to be severely reprimanded by one of the girls who turned out to a friend of the Fred Pontin family. Within minutes they had vanished and returned with three rather large security guards, who were quick to eject both Pat and Don. The incident failed to deter them—they simply pitched their tent outside the camp and regained illegal entry the following morning, enjoying a further three days with Paddy and friends. The two lads also gained the bonus of a chalet floor to sleep on, having met up with a group of boys who invited them to share their accommodation. It was not the only holiday camp experience that Pat was to have with Don; just a few years later he was asked yet again to bend the truth in support of his friend's single-minded drive and ambition.

The years at St Philip's provided far more than an academic education for Don although eventually he emerged quite content with his achievements in that realm. Whilst he did not achieve passes in all his 'O' levels subjects a year early, as had been intended, he was offered the chance to re-sit some the following year, along with others of his own age group. There was little doubt that Don had taken full advantage of every opportunity offered to him both inside and outside the classroom. Life had been lived to the full in every way and, in his mind, he saw no reason why it shouldn't continue in his working life beyond school. But the passage from one environment to the next proved far more difficult than he had ever imagined.

4

Seven 'O' Levels and a Life-Saving Certificate

'How do you catch the wind and tie it down?' is a well-known line from *The Sound of Music*. It may well have been the question on the lips of certain senior staff in the Inland Revenue office in Birmingham at the start of the sixties. The 'wind' in this case was a lively, boisterous sixteen-year-old Don Maclean, trying to start his working life in an environment that required peace, tranquillity, orderliness, a desire to be desk-bound and an appetite for facts and figures. The Civil Service and Don Maclean were clearly incompatible. His noisy, fast and furious people-centred outlook on life caused such disruption that his departure eighteen months later brought great relief on both sides.

After five busy and satisfying years at St Philip's Grammar School Don was full of enthusiasm and ambition. Success on the sports field, in the classroom and on stage had given him tremendous confidence with which to go out into the working world. Only a minority stayed on into the sixth form to study for university entrance and having already achieved a very acceptable standard of results at 'O' level the question of a further two years at school never really arose. The only distraction to what looked to be a positive future for Don was the concern he had for his mother, who had been unwell for a number of weeks. This fear stemmed largely from not knowing what was wrong with her, which was made all the more difficult by his father's reluctance to discuss the illness. As a result of Charles Maclean's preoccupation with his wife's condition, Don was left to make his own decisions about the future. Along with the majority of his year group, he was keen to be earning a living and so pursued the vast range of job opportunities and apprenticeships available in the early sixties. The climate of the times was one of optimism and opportunity, made all the more secure for Don by the seven valuable 'O' levels and a life-saving qualification to his credit. His final choice was what he thought would be a safe, stable and secure job with plenty of promotion opportunities: the Civil Service.

The Inland Revenue had not been his first choice of departments. Customs and Excises had attracted him to the Civil Service in the first instance but he could not enter that particular section until he was eighteen. It was with a degree of reluctance that he agreed to work for those two years in the tax office, ensuring that the citizens of Smethick paid as they earned. But the transition from school to this particular working environment was not an easy one. He felt a complete misfit. The whole atmosphere restrained his natural personality, slowly and painfully suppressing the real Don Maclean. Working in a mixed-sex environment also presented him with problems he had not anticipated. St Philip's all-boys school and male teachers had not prepared him for ambitious, strong-willed women who were enjoying the privileges of equal opportunities at work. The Civil Service had been one of the first employers to provide equal pay for women as well as welcome promotion, consequently attracting many. Don had only ever encountered women as mothers, primary school teachers and nuns and this experience was difficult to adjust to. He could not relate to the

female conversation and resented the endless stream of col-
lections for birthdays, anniversaries, hospital patients and
flowers at the end of each week. There were many Fridays when
he wondered if he'd go home with any wages left at all.

He tried as hard as he could to raise a laugh, lighten the
atmosphere and provoke humour wherever possible but it was
an uphill struggle all the way. His singing and humming only
produced a reaction of *ssshh* and jokes died a painful death. The
people he worked with were not especially funny although a
number of them became excellent resource material for his
future act. One of the chief inspectors summed up Don's time in
his department with the parting words: ' In all the time you have
been here you have never conducted yourself in a true Civil
Service-like manner.' Eighteen months was all that he could
endure and so instead of gravitating towards Customs and
Excise he planned his escape to a holiday camp.

Despite his success in the Birmingham parks tent
competitions and children's talent shows Don had never seriously considered a life in show business; he had never thought
it possible to earn a living from the thing that he enjoyed doing
most. When on stage he thrived on the affection he could gain
from a responsive audience but had never seen it as anything
but an enjoyable hobby which had occasionally paid his
expenses. The Inland Revenue experience changed all that.
Whether it was a sudden belief in his own talent or the
desperation to get out of a bad situation he's not sure but he
found enough confidence and courage to write to the Warner's
holiday camp at Seaton where he had spent so many happy
family holidays with his parents. In a carefully composed letter
he set about the task of selling his talents and skills for a
summer job. Knowing from first-hand experience just what was
required, he highlighted his sporting abilities and the
invaluable life-saving certificate he had acquired at school;
every camp needed life guards with recognized qualifications
and his love of and experiences in entertaining came second. All

the effort put into the application was not in vain. The reply came not from Seaton but the headquarters of Warner Brothers, offering him the job of sports organizer at their small Northney camp on Hayling Island. The location was unimportant to Don. It was his passport out of the tax office and he grabbed it with both hands.

The summer of 1961 is engraved upon Don's memory. Bursting with confidence and the sense of freedom he arrived along with all the other Greencoats a week before the campers, in order to prepare the holiday programme. At the first team meeting they learned that the camp comedian and entertainments manager had backed out of his contract to work at Northney; a better offer had come his way. Camp officials had no time in which to re-advertise or audition and so were looking towards one of the existing team to take on the job. There weren't many seconds of silence before the least experienced, most newly appointed sports organizer stepped forward and announced, 'I volunteer, sir.' It was to be one of the quickest promotions, albeit self-promotion, of Don Maclean's life. One minute he was mentally planning children's games and a swimming gala, the next accepting full responsibility for organizing the entire camp's entertainment programme. It involved arranging the weekly concert, singing, acting as host to numerous events and activities as well as overseeing the infamous camp beauty competitions—which he clearly remembers doing so in a Tarzan outfit. A blend of youthful naivety and confident talent produced the required goods. The family audiences loved him, his act and his ability to produce quality entertainment all week for sixteen weeks of the season. Needless to say the camp officials were also delighted with their new found protégé.

At the end of the season Don left Hayling Island convinced that he was God's gift to the world of entertainment. As far as he could see, overnight success was just around the corner. But his false sense of security was shortly to be shattered. Clutching numerous telephone numbers and names of contacts and agents he made his way up to London, in order to seek his next responsive audience. First on his list was the Windmill Theatre, a small theatre in Great Windmill Street, off Shaftesbury Avenue. During the post war years it had become a showcase for agents, managers and BBC producers to view certain acts, particularly comedians. In its early days it had specialized in nude and dance shows. In between these scenes the proprietor would put on comedians. It was tough training for a would-be comic as the audience came for the nudity rather than the jokes and they did six shows a day, starting before noon. But at this time it still remained one of the few ways in which to be seen by prospective employers of comedians. Don knew that many of his heroes enjoying success in radio comedy, such as Harry Secombe, Peter Sellers and Dick Emery, had all started at the Windmill. Auditions were held regularly; he went with enthusiasm and high hopes but was not to be added to that number.

The experience remains vivid in his memory. His act had developed into a wide range of impressions including people such as Chic Murray, Al Read and Jerry Lewis. On this particular occasion he took the stage before his adjudicator who appeared to be slumped somewhere in the centre of the stalls with feet propped up on the seat in front. Don commenced but the response was minimal. The body seemingly sank further into the seat causing the feet to rise higher. Halfway through the act a loud, expressionless voice penetrated the darkness saying, 'That's enough, thank you.' At first the comment was insufficient to quell the young comedian's confidence. He jokingly responded, 'I haven't finished yet, I'm only halfway through!' and proceeded with the act. The second time round the slumped body made himself quite clear. In a cold and cutting tone he announced, 'Would you kindly leave the stage.' A chastened and dispirited Don Maclean did so. The real road into the world of entertainment was beginning to reveal itself.

The slide from his holiday camp mountain-top experience into the valley of rejection had been fast and painful. Unbeknown to him he had joined a long list of comedians including Spike Milligan, Roy Castle and Benny Hill, all of whom had failed the Windmill audition.

On his return home to Birmingham it was suggested that he try his hand at teaching, a decision which delighted his father. Those seriously considering entering the profession were often offered student teacher positions for a year, in order to test their vocation before starting teacher training college. Don remembers feeling surprised that all he had to do was take a medical and manage to keep one or two steps ahead of his pupils, some of whom turned out to be only a few years younger than himself. A local Birmingham secondary modern school took him on a year's contract to teach biology, one of his best Grammar School subjects. The experience was a productive one in that, after only a few weeks, he knew for certain that teaching was not for him and he had no intentions of spending the rest of his days in a classroom. With the Windmill Theatre experience only weeks behind him, the entertainment bug surfaced again and once more he planned his escape. Half-term saw him make the trek up to London for yet another audition, with the Robert Leighton Agency in Long Acre.

The secretary of the agency was embarrassed when Don arrived, knowing that he had travelled down early in the morning in time for the prearranged audition. Her boss was ill and there was no one available to deal with the enthusiastic young performer. In an attempt to soften the blow she took him around the corner to the Max Rivers studio in Newport Street where she knew auditions were taking place for a pantomime due to be staged in Southend later that year. The two men responsible for the auditions were Jerry Jerome—a large comic—and Marty Swift. Jerry Jerome owned the company and was producing the show as well as playing the role of dame whilst Marty Swift had already been cast in the principal comedy role for the pantomime. The secretary hoped that they might listen to Don's act and offer her some advice as to whether the agency should put him on its books or not. Don felt relaxed and the audition went well. They were encouraging and responsive, laughing at the gags and generally creating an environment in which Don could perform confidently. He did and they did far more than recommend him to the agents: they hired him themselves for the Southend pantomime season. They actually went to the trouble of writing in a small part for him which although way down the bill, became the first of many pantomimes that were the mainstay of his career. He had no difficulty in handing his notice in at school for the end of that autumn term, having firmly crossed teaching off his list of future career possibilities. He was lifting himself out of the valley and back onto the road, with sights clearly set for a life in show business.

Enthusiasm and youthful confidence rather than experience or skill got him through the pantomime season. He thrived on the atmosphere, loving every single minute of his time spent performing. But he also knew that his own contribution was poor in comparison to those of the others with whom he shared the stage. Don could see just how much he had to learn and how enthusiasm alone would not further his career. His time at Southend helped him to appreciate that his chosen profession required hard work and commitment. He knew that he had the necessary talents and set about the task of acquiring some recognizable professional training that would help him on his way.

The season came to an end all too quickly, providing ample time for the now unemployed Don Maclean to research the possibilities of drama and theatre schools. He was left feeling unsure of exactly what he wanted to do on stage—sing, act seriously or continue along the impressionist comedy line that he had already started on. However his attempt to register as unemployed at one of the Birmingham labour exchanges provided a powerful incentive to succeed in one way or another. As soon as the clerk at the counter saw that he had had eighteen months' experience in the Inland Revenue he was offered a job in the Labour Exchange in place of unemployment benefit. It served a useful dual purpose. First, it was a means of earning some money and second, a powerful reminder of the work environment that had driven him away to the world of show business in the first place. Grateful for the much-needed income he accepted the position, which was only made bearable in the light of the knowledge that he had been awarded both a grant and a place at theatre school for the coming September.

The Birmingham Theatre School headed up by Mary Richard offered a two-year course of considerable variety. Theatre trends of the time meant that young people set on a stage career had to be able to turn their hand to a song and dance as well as straight acting. Over the years this particular school had sought to meet the demands of the day in providing a course that would offer training in song, dance, mime, straight acting and variety entertainment. It allowed students such as Don to try their hand at everything, as well as specializing in their chosen discipline. And Don did try everything. His performances in Shakespeare plays as well as being compère of variety shows received the praise and encouragement of all his teachers. One in particular, Eileen Knight, was especially fond of him. She had spent considerable time as a performer in variety theatre and musicals herself and recognized Don's talents immediately. She encouraged him in every way that she could, providing plenty of opportunities for him to write material, direct and perform. Revue-type shows became a regular feature of college life during his two years and their success regularly drew the attention of the local press. On a more traditional note Don also appeared in several Shakespearean productions, in which he regularly sought out the comedy roles such as the gatekeeper in *Macbeth*, the gravedigger in *Hamlet* and the gardener in *Richard II*.

Theatre School provided the time, space and opportunity for Don to experiment with his talents and make an un-pressured decision as to which strand of the world of enter-tainment he really wanted to enter. It also gave him the chance to perform in roles that he knew he would never have the opportunity to play elsewhere. But by far the most valuable thing that he gained from these two years was the friendship and companionship of a group of students who lived and breathed drama and literature. In contrast to the year that followed Don, his contemporaries at the school were older and mature students. They gained somewhat of a reputation for being a snobbish group that set themselves apart from other years but it was the love and passion for their subject that bound them together. They spent hours debating and discussing all aspects of literature and drama.

Five pounds a week was a generous grant at that time but considerably less than the salary Don had been earning both at the holiday camp and in pantomime. By still living at home in Sparkbrook with his parents he was able to live more comfortably than most students but he still kept an eye open for vacation work to supplement his income. An advertisement in *The Stage* newspaper attracted his attention during his first term at theatre school. The company were advertising for a bass singer to join a chorus booked to do four weeks of pantomime in Southampton. He was delighted to discover that the auditions were taking place at the Max River Studios where he had been so successful only a year earlier. History repeated itself and Don was offered the job. Ron Wayne was responsible for his appointment and became both a friend and mentor to Don during that time. Top of the bill—in what was a much bigger show than he had experienced before—were Joan Regan and Richard Hearne, better known as Mr Pastry from the popular children's television programme 'Mr Pastry' of the late fifties and early sixties. Joan Regan befriended many of the younger artists, offering praise, encouragement and support wherever she could. On one occasion she even lent Don her car to visit a friend in London. It was a happy second pantomime season for Don, adding to his valuable list of work experience.

Only six months later, that list lengthened once more as an invitation arrived from Warners' camps for Don to take a more senior camp entertainment officer's position at their largest site in Minster on the Isle of Sheppey, in Kent. It filled the theatre school summer vacation nicely and removed any fear of the possibility of having to return to work at the Labour Exchange, albeit temporarily. Once more the relaxed family holiday atmosphere fuelled Don's confidence as he thrived on everything from organizing afternoon hikes to Saturday night variety performances. His own act was fast developing from just impressions to include general comedy routines and a con-siderable amount of singing. There appeared to be no holding him back and he was invited to return for a further season the following year. He took full advantage of his senior position in helping his old school friend Pat Barr find a summer job before going off to university. Pat was impressed with his friend's success and influence but somewhat taken back when, on his arrival, Don gave him strict instructions to tell anyone who might ask, that both of them were twenty-one years of age. Fortunately the need did not arise but Pat often wondered how many holiday camps entertainment programmes were being organized by eighteen year olds.

Don's time at Minster provided him with invaluable experience in a positive and friendly atmosphere. But it wasn't his only gain from that time. On the first day of his second season at Minster he recognized a pretty face from the previous year belonging to a young attractive Anglo-French girl by the name of Antoinette Roux. She was to become his wife.

5

Toni

The Warner Brothers' Minster site was Bet and Tom Roux's first experience of a holiday camp. It had taken their daughter Toni (short for Antoinette) some time to convince them to try it. Having experienced the atmosphere for herself when working as a Redcoat on a Butlin's site in Ayr, Scotland, she was sure that they would enjoy it. They were finally persuaded when she offered to go with them and her youngest sister and they were not disappointed. Their fears of being pressured into an endless stream of activities were completely allayed as the whole holiday turned out to be a thoroughly enjoyable experience for both parents and their two youngest daughters. As a result they made immediate plans to return the following year. There was little doubt in their minds as to the invaluable contribution made by one young man.

The whole family had been very impressed with the handsome young camp entertainments officer, Don Maclean. Knowing something of the demands of the life of a Redcoat, Toni had admired his skills in handling people, helping them to relax and get the best out of their holiday. In addition to these essential requirements Don had displayed a whole host of additional talents. Toni had offered very few specialized skills when applying for the position in Ayr and had found the demands of entertaining holiday-makers all day long a welcome challenge. The red jacket and white skirt marked you out wherever you went on the campsite and you were expected to respond to a wide range of requests and situations. The experience helped bring her out of her shell, overcoming a shyness of meeting strangers and over the weeks her confidence had grown, particularly in relating to men and boys. Coming from a family of four girls she had limited experience of mixing and socializing with members of the opposite sex. Most of the young men she had dated were all well scrutinized by her strict but caring father. Her two elder sisters were already happily married and her parents had every intention of helping her and her younger sister make a right choice of life partner too.

Don made the task of entertaining look so easy and Toni knew that was an art in itself. During the day he'd arrange competitions and games, take campers on hikes and walks and still find the energy to organize and compère the evening programmes, often doing his own solo spot as part of it. His infectious personality, boundless energy and broad and cheeky grin won the hearts of all the holidaymakers. Toni's admiration had been very much from a distance during their first visit to Minster. They finally exchanged just a very few words on the last day as they were preparing to leave. Don helped the family to carry their cases and they took the opportunity of thanking him for all his hard work during their stay. Tom took a snapshot of the family standing together with Don before they departed. As they journeyed home Toni distinctly remembers her father saying that he was the kind of young man he'd like to see her marry one day.

Don's day off was usually a Saturday when the camp emptied and refilled again. He had a good arrangement with the baggage boys who were responsible for carrying the campers' luggage to their chalets. If they noted a particularly attractive young lady they would be sure to remember the chalet number and inform Don. On this particular day they told him to look out for two good-looking sisters in B block. It wasn't until they met up later that evening that Don realized just who one of the sisters was.

No one was more amazed than Toni when during the introductory welcome evening for team and guests Don made a beeline for her saying, 'Hello, you were here last year, weren't you?' She had remembered him but was astonished that following such a brief encounter on their last day he had remembered her. It didn't take them long to arrange to meet for a walk later that evening, after he had finished his duty. There was little doubt in Don's mind that this was love at second, if not first sight. She was a stunningly beautiful girl with a lively spirit about her and he had decided that if he didn't invite her out straight away someone else might get in before him. Toni's reactions were not quite so clear-cut. She was undoubtedly attracted to him but knowing how certain Redcoats at Butlins had operated with young women on holiday she was just a touch cautious. She had no intentions of becoming someone's convenient holiday romance, only to be dumped at the end of the week in exchange for one of the following week's guests.

Don's only disappointment on that first walk together was the fact that Toni had changed out of the attractive blue and white checked dress with a long pointed collar, in which she had looked stunning, into jeans and a very hairy mohair jumper. He also noticed a rather unusual attachment to her jeans right through the top waist button. It was a very large baby's nappy pin. Intrigued by the fact that its presence was very obvious and there appeared to be no attempt to hide or cover it up Don asked Toni why it was there. There was no hesitation in her reply. 'I've experienced you holiday camp entertainers before and know what you lot are like,' she said unashamedly. Don got the message loud and clear.

As the week progressed it was hard for Toni not to show just how interested she was in Don. She was quite clear in her own mind of what she wanted from a relationship and he was fulfilling her highest hopes. She was tired of young men who had bored her to tears with their lack of interest and conversation and of those for whom a good-night kiss appeared to be the beginning, middle and end of a date. On their very first walk out together the conversation hadn't stopped. They exchanged likes and dislikes, opinions on films, music, the theatre and plays they had both enjoyed. They learned just how similar their home upbringing had been, sharing strong moral values, family loyalty, a simple lifestyle and the influence of the Christian faith. The list of topics was endless—and a good-night kiss no less enjoyable. During the week they arranged to see each other as much as Don's job allowed, dragging out the off-duty time as much as they could. Each evening Don walked Toni back to the chalet that she shared with her younger sister. One particular night he called in to collect an apple pie that he had inadvertently left behind during the day, which the camp cook had baked especially for him. Toni's mother happened to call in at that very moment to see if the girls were alright. She was not amused to see Don in the chalet at that time of the evening. In no uncertain terms she made her feelings known.

'And what do you think you are doing in here, young man?' she bellowed. An unusually embarrassed and nervous Don replied, 'I've only come for me apple pie.'

'Take your apple pie and go!' instructed Bet.

The phrase, 'Take your pie and go!' was to become a standing family joke in the future but right then it was a loud and clear message from a caring mother as to exactly how any boyfriend of her daughter was expected to behave. Don did not disappoint them.

Toni continued to remain guarded as the week's holiday came to an end. The promises of weekly visits to Pimlico from Minster on his one day off a week were about to be tested. For the remaining period of the holiday camp season Don made that weekly journey to take Toni out for the evening. Any fears she might have had concerning his sincerity were soon alleviated. Their relationship flourished with the distinct approval of the whole Roux family. Bet and Tom seemed completely undisturbed by the fact that he was just a student training for a profession that had no guaranteed future security. His warm, affectionate personality combined with a determined, hard- working character was more than enough to win their affections. Toni felt quite sure that her father secretly admired the courage Don had in being prepared to take risks, doing what he had wanted rather than what was always expected of him. In the years that followed Tom was, without doubt, Don's biggest fan, always believing in his talent as well as his ability to care for his daughter.

As the holiday camp season came to an end the weekly evening visits extended to weekends, as Don returned to Birmingham and theatre school. They became very familiar with the strip of motorway between the two cities as they pursued a courtship of almost four years. Toni continued to work in the offices of a London-based airline company, frequently travelling to the Midlands to accompany Don on his weekend club engagements. Her sights were firmly set on marriage and she waited patiently until Don decided not so much whether they should get married but when. Since they had met when he was only twenty years of age he had wanted to wait a few years before taking on the responsibility and commitment of marriage. It was a decision made for life and one they were both to take very seriously indeed. When that time came Don did the dutiful and expected thing in formally asking Tom Roux for his daughter's hand in marriage and nothing could have pleased the man more than having Don as a son-in-law. 11 February 1967 was a day of great celebration for all who knew them and the start of a life together that has enjoyed almost thirty years' friendship and partnership in marriage.

The ceremony took place at All Souls Roman Catholic Church, Pimlico. Bet Roux had been brought up in the Methodist Church whilst Tom, even though he had French roots, had a Church of England background. His grandfather fought in the French Infantry but died of wounds inflicted at

Arras, just a month before Tom's father was born. It was soon after his grandfather's death that the family moved to London and Tom spent the rest of his time growing up in the Pimlico area where he met and married Bet. Toni had been sent along to a Sunday school as a child but had spent most of her adult worshipping days in an Anglo-Catholic church in Pimlico enjoying the high mass tradition, so worshipping at a Roman Catholic church with Don was not a problem for her. She recognized very early on in their relationship just how central Don's faith was to his life and how much it was the making of him as a person; the two were clearly inseparable. Her love for Don meant acceptance of his faith. Before and after their marriage they always found time to attend mass together. The one thing that she knew she could be sure of was, should they be blessed with children, they would never be sent to church but taken. That pleased her more than anything.

There was very little that Toni didn't know about the world of show business by the time they were married. She had entered into this commitment with her eyes well and truly open. Supporting Don through his last year at theatre school and doing the rounds of the clubs with him had been as much an education for her as for him. Many a weekend had been spent in Coventry or another nearby town clutching half a shandy and a bag of crisps as she watched him try out his rapidly changing act on largely sceptical audiences. It was a rude awakening from the positive and happy atmosphere of the holiday camp where he simply could not fail to please his public. The clubs of the sixties had more than their fair share of highly opinionated individuals who never failed to make their feelings known. Don fought hard to win over his audiences whoever or wherever they were and Toni played her part from the sidelines. When jokes died she'd laugh hysterically and provide him with the useful one-liner, 'that's the wife, you know—thanks luv' whilst he quickly changed tack in search of a better response. She learned to sense the atmosphere of an audience and judge quite accurately before a show as to how hard it would be for Don on stage. He always valued her comments and feedback, both the encouragement and the criticism for he knew the latter would be constructive with his best interest at heart. They were in the business together, right from the start, one enjoying the limelight and the other content with soft side lights. Only one appeared on stage but it was clearly a double act, a partnership that was proving both successful and enjoyable. The lifestyle that emerged was very different from that of many newly-weds but became the norm for Toni. Even when the opportunity arose for Don to work during their honeymoon, she was delighted.

Her work with an airline company provided them with affordable flights to Australia for what turned out to be a working honeymoon. It was not Toni's first visit to the continent, as she had visited her sister and husband who had emigrated some years earlier. The February wedding had been scheduled to fit between pantomime and summer season but Don did not immediately disclose to his agent the real reason for wanting three weeks clear of work. When the truth did emerge, nobody was more surprised than Don when it was suggested that he might combine honeymoon with cabaret. Realizing how useful the money would be for them he agreed to pursue the possibility.

Following three nights in a Sydney honeymoon hotel, the newly-weds went to stay with Toni's eldest sister Pat and her husband from where they arranged to work for Percy and Jenny King at the Granville Retired Soldiers League. The couple agreed to squeeze Don's short act into the programme for a few nights but said that they could not offer more than a $50 fee per night. Don and Toni both managed to hide their reaction until they were out of sight: the figure was double anything Don had ever earned in the United Kingdom. They were delighted—and so were the Australian audiences. Don's short, sharp and snappy style was quite new to them and all his material refreshingly unfamiliar. The combination worked well and the few nights turned into weeks. The newly-weds thrived on the hospitality of Australian people, the climate and the pay. Not only did they delight in being able to afford to buy new clothes and souvenirs but succeeded in returning home with more money than they had gone out with. Australia is the only place in the world, apart from Birmingham, that Don has ever felt an inclination towards making his home. His first experience of the people and place was sufficiently strong to make him seriously consider emigrating. But on this occasion they did not have that chance as both knew they had to return to their new house, their families and their work commitments. The three week honeymoon came to an end all too soon.

The months and years leading up to their wedding had been spent saving hard for a new house in the Selly Oak area of Birmingham. Don was adamant that he shouldn't have to live in London in order to succeed in show business and reluctant to look anywhere other than his home city. Only the pull of the world of working men's clubs had made them fleetingly consider living in Doncaster, Yorkshire but Birmingham finally won the day. They had watched their small but brand new home being built, frequently donning wellingtons in order to view the latest layer of brickwork, window or door frame and finally the roof. Their only disappointment came when they were told that the house was unlikely to be ready in time for their return from Australia. Reluctantly they agreed to a temporary separation and rejoined their respective parents for a short time until its completion.

Despite the luxury of their Australian profits, times were hard financially. Toni continued to work in order to supplement Don's somewhat erratic earnings, at first temping for different firms but eventually securing a permanent position at the conveniently located university in Selly Oak. Their lifestyle was simple; they existed without many household items until they could afford them, even to the degree of surviving without carpets or cooker for several months after their wedding. An electric frying pan that Toni had purchased before they were married became the sole source of cooking. Even when their income did increase, they were both cautious about over-spending on unnecessary items. Consequently they lived for many years without such luxuries as a refrigerator or a washing machine. Material possessions were not important to them. Don had wanted to have the security of owning his own home but the quality of their relationship and time spent together had a far greater priority than anything they could buy for their house.

Toni continued to accompany Don on his evening and weekend work commitments but the pressures of this and holding down a full-time job soon exhausted her. Some nights, after travelling home from one of the clubs in the Potteries, she would spend just three or four hours in bed before getting up for work. Don would then collect her for lunch when she found herself dashing around doing the domestic chores so that her evenings were clear to accompany him to work. The strain was too great and she decided she would rather budget even more tightly in order to be with Don than earn additional money. Toni handed in her notice at the university. It was a decision that created the framework for the rest of their lives together and one that they have never regretted.

Toni shared in the joys and frustrations of the business with her husband. There was never a night that Don went on stage without realizing that she, in so very many ways, had put him there. Rosie Maclean had been a doting mother and had done little to prepare her son for the world of domesticity. When he had been living at home she regularly got up at two and three 'o'clock in the morning as he returned from the clubs in order to cook for him. Don's expectation were high in the domestic realm and Toni whilst drawing the line at 3a.m. meals did not disappoint him. During the early years there were times when she even made his stage clothes as well as washing and ironing them. Packing became one of the more domestic skills that Don did master. But Toni was far more than a domestic aid to the business. Her constant companionship and involvement in the development of the act was of great importance to Don. He saw little point in being married unless they were together sharing in each other's lives. Only a few months after she had taken the decision to finish work, a gift of a job opportunity came Don's way, providing them with a stable and guaranteed income for forty-eight weeks. They travelled the length and breadth of Britain together, with the White Heather Club. It was a happy time, offering Don both good experience and exposure and it became his passport out of the world of working men's clubs. He had become increasingly unhappy about the pressure upon him to produce unsavoury and 'blue' material in that environment and was relieved no longer to be dependent upon it as a source of income. It was also the time when their first child, Rachel Heather, was born. Her middle name was chosen as an expression of their thankfulness for this particularly happy period in their working and family life.

During the week prior to Rachel's birth Don had been working in Wimbledon with the White Heather Club and living with Bet and Tom in Pimlico. Bet Roux was very concerned that her daughter should return home in plenty of time for the birth but Toni felt quite relaxed wherever she was and confident that a baby could be born anywhere provided they were in easy reach of a hospital. In the event both parents were in Birmingham but for Don, it was only just. Toni went into labour late one afternoon whilst he was working in Hull. She telephoned to say that she was taking herself into hospital. Don did the evening show and drove straight to be with her. On his arrival he was informed that she had been given an injection and would not be producing her baby until the following morning. Grateful for the night's sleep Don went home and returned early the next morning, hoping to be able to be with Toni for the birth. Unfortunately for him the delivery room had two beds in it and there was another woman about to give birth; consequently he was unable to go in. Rachel was born at 11a.m. on 19 March 1969. He managed a quick cuddle, made two phone calls to the new grandparents and drove back to Hull for the show.

Don was a proud parent who had every intention of being the best father he could. Being around during the day meant that he could share in every part of caring for Rachel. What he may have lacked in household domesticity he made up for in childcare skills. Much to his mother's amazement—and, at times, unhappiness—Don became as proficient at feeding, bathing and nappy changing as Toni was. As an only child he had had very little experience of small children and babies but proved to be a fast learner. The principle of being together, adopted very early in their marriage, was now extended to include Rachel. There was no way in which any of them were prepared to be without each other a day longer than was necessary, so within the first year of her life Rachel learned to travel and continued to do so for many years to come.

Some of their accommodation wasn't always what they had wanted. One particular pantomime season in Bradford remains firmly fixed in both their memories. Bradford in York-shire isn't the warmest place on a summer's day and this particular winter was long and hard. A friend had been kind enough to offer a relatives house for the Macleans to use during their stay. It was small and basic, with limited electricity and coal fires as the only source of warmth. Arriving just a few days before Christmas, Don was busy with rehearsals whilst Toni tried to make the little house into a home for them. It wasn't until late on Christmas Eve that they ventured out into the coal shed, only to discover that there had not been a delivery of coal, as they had been led to believe, and they had absolutely no source of heat at all. The situation was made far worst by the fact that Toni was obviously sickening for something. Don spent his Christmas morning walking around Bradford in search of a petrol station that might just sell him some coal for the fire. It was not an experience that any of them wished to repeat.

Due to Toni's illness for the following few days Don took nine-month-old Rachel into Bradford's Alhambra Theatre, where she was entertained by various members of the cast according to whether or not they were on stage. Vince Hill topped the bill on that occasion and Toni clearly remembers the support and kindness offered by him and his wife Ann. He never distinguished between the top and bottom of the bill. They were all valued and appreciated for themselves as individuals and were treated alike. She recalls saying to Don at the end of that season, 'If you ever make top of the bill I hope that you will be just like Vince.' On this occasion Don and Toni were on the receiving end of the support of their ever-increasing showbusiness family. But in the years to come it wasn't just Don who would offer a warm and family type atmosphere behind stage but Toni too. Together they have become the support and 'family' to many others in the business.

6

Climbing Towards the Top

Don's sights were now firmly set on succeeding in the world of entertainment. Having experienced one or two knocks and discouragements early on he was well aware of the steep climb ahead of him and he was confident in his abilities although he knew that in order to reach the very top he'd require far more endurance and determination than talent. It would have been a mistake to attempt the climb without the talent but foolish to try without the determination necessary to keep going. He was beginning to realize that success in show business had more to do with finding the lucky breaks than being the best. Experience so far had shown that there was plenty of talent around but very little opportunity for it to be seen.

By the time he left Birmingham Theatre School in the summer of 1964 Don had three summer seasons, two panto-mimes, several straight acting roles and three years of club work behind him. He was also in the privileged position of being able to turn both full time and professional in the business. 1964 was the year of his coming of age: he was just twenty-one years old. For someone who had only thought seriously about show business three years earlier it was a pretty impressive start, displaying many of the qualities he would need in the hard climb ahead.

At this early stage of his career Don was pleased to have been offered a professional start to that ascent. He found himself in the privileged position of having to choose between two jobs, a decision that did not prove too difficult. Not all of his Shakespeare performances could have gone unnoticed, as Sheffield Playhouse offered him six pounds and ten shillings a week for playing small parts in a production of *Anthony and Cleopatra* in conjunction with the assistant stage manager's job. The second offer could not have been more of a contrast. One of the well-known producers of the day, Ted Dwyer, invited Don to join his company as an all-round entertainer for the summer season production of *Follies on Parade* at Skegness Pier. Mr Dwyer was also offering eighteen pounds a week pay. With little hesitation Don packed his bags for Skegness for his first officially recognized professional engagement. The Birmingham Theatre School were not surprised by his early success in securing such a position. He had developed numerous skills as an all-round entertainer over the last few years, many of which had been clearly recognized in the school's end-of-year revue show. The critics from the local press had been positive and encouraging:

> *The compère Don Maclean had a nice line in comedy, a polished technique and a flair for mimicry, which though there was nothing particularly original about his performance, augers well for a professional career which starts soon.*

Don knew just how important it was to do well on this first official summer season. Each job might well become his passport to the next. Contacts made and reviews received by the press were enormous factors in determining the next step of his journey. Ted Dwyer, often described as the Peter Pan of the seaside, had produced fifteen consecutive years of summer seasons at the Pier Theatre in Skegness, providing shows with an emphasis on 'good, clean family entertainment to suit all tastes'.

It was a good company to be part of and Don joined an experienced and proven cast including comedian Stan Waite and a popular vocalist of the day, Brian Grey. The pace was relentless but it was an excellent training ground, with twelve performances a week including five different programmes throughout the season, plus a completely separate weekly Old Time Music Hall programme. In addition to his nightly solo impressionist spot Don took part in numerous skits and sketches, songs and choruses. He took the stage in one way or another for more than half of the eighteen items listed on each of the five different programmes. He thrived on the experience and so did the audiences. Both local and national theatre critics gave credit to the young performer's appearances. Many journalists singled out his individual contributions, leaving few doubts as to how well Ted Dwyer's newcomer had been received.

> *... my favourite for the evening was Don Maclean with his natural flair for funnies and a couple of good impersonations of Ted Lune and Jerry Lewis. His versatile voice gave much to the whole evening's performance.*

> *Then came the hilarious high spot of the evening when the whole audience were in hysterics for all of five minutes as Don Maclean modelled a vintage swimsuit. Just standing there without a move, Don could have forced laughter from Scrooge.*

Such was his success with the Lincolnshire holiday-makers that when vocalist Brian Grey took ill with laryngitis Don was offered his higher spot on the bill. The audience were delighted to get a double dose of the 'handsome newcomer whose personality wins him as much applause as his material,' to quote that particular week's review. It was no surprise when, long before the end of that first season, Ted Dwyer invited him to return the following year. Don accepted his offer immediately. It had been a tremendous start to his professional career.

There was another personal highlight for Don at Skegness. It came on his Sunday night off, when one of his radio heroes Ted Ray appeared at the Arcadia to do a one-night show. It was the first opportunity that Don had ever had to watch Ted perform live and he was determined to make the most of it. It came at a stage when he was working hard to develop his own individual style as a comedian. Inevitably he was influenced by many of his different favourite comedians but Ted Ray topped Don's personal bill in those days. Sunday nights became an important component in his process of observation and analysis, part of the ambitious task of finding a style that he hoped would, one day, single him out as an equally successful and individual performer.

Soon after the end of the Skegness summer season a surprising television offer came his way. Soap operas were few and far between in the sixties although the Midlands' answer to the successful Manchester-based Coronation Street was an equally popular programme called 'Crossroads'. Following the saga of a family-owned motel business it attracted millions of viewers several nights a week and was a particular favourite of Midlanders themselves. Many stars in the world of enter-tainment had appeared on the programme at one time or another, so when the invitation came his way Don accepted it gladly.

He was offered two weeks as Cy Townsend, the comic bass player in a pop group called Georgie Saint and the Dragons. He thoroughly enjoyed his first experience of television acting. Midlanders also enjoyed seeing a local boy on their programme. Don's only regret came some months later when the producers decided to revive the character and offered him a further thirteen-week contract which he was unable to accept, having signed to return to Skegness for a second season. He often wonders if his career might have turned in a very different direction had he been able to accept the second 'Crossroads' contract.

The end of the summer season and the short-lived television opportunity took Don back to the clubs where he had gained much of his experience and experimented with the style and variety of his act over the last few years. He worked alongside many of the big names on the club scene at that time including Dukes and Lee, Lynne Perry (Ivy from 'Coronation Street') and Norman Collier who was enjoying tremendous success. It had taken Don some time and perseverance to develop a style that he felt comfortable with as a performer and he found that he was gradually emerging more as a stand-up comic than the impressionist that he had started out as. He often sang as part of the act and in the early days would accompany himself on a guitar. The clubs allowed him the freedom to experiment although they were not always as polite or complimentary as summer season holiday-makers. There were no floodlights or orchestra pit to separate you from the audience in a club; you were on intimate terms right from the start. Many were there simply to chat with their friends or have a drink, the entertainment being secondary in their minds. It was a challenge that Don accepted each time he went out to perform and the more difficult the audience the harder he worked to win them over. There were just a few occasions on which he reluctantly gave up; he recalls one particular night vividly.

The club was situated somewhere on the Wolverhampton Road not too far from his Birmingham home. He had been practising a new routine which, on this occasion, he had decided to hold in reserve just in case he got stuck. Not being over-familiar with the words he had written them on the inside of the flat cap that he was wearing as part of the stage act. Desperation set in halfway through the performance, as he had failed to draw a single laugh from the audience since the beginning of the act. Off came the cap in search of what he'd hoped would be a life-saving prompt. To his horror the carefully secured script was smeared all over with warm, greasy brylcreem from his head. The words were illegible and the paper had become transparent. As a result he dried up on stage. His desperate attempt to save the act failed miserably and he walked off, having clearly 'died' on that occasion. His lasting memory is of the club secretary muttering behind him, 'I keep telling that Dave Kenton [the agent] to stop sending me bloody crap like you.'

A one-night stand in a Northern miners' club remains permanently fixed in Don's memory as the most traumatic experience in this early part of his career. He was quite used to having to work hard with an audience and on several occasions had lived through the pain of 'dying' but this particular night he felt condemned to the grave before the end of his first gag. The evening got off to a bad start when he was informed that he was the only act booked and faced the daunting prospect of appearing several times throughout the evening. It became apparent from the outset that his material and style was not what the miners wanted. (Whilst aware that this audience required a very different act to the one he offered during summer and pantomime seasons Don had always resisted the temptation to colour his work blue like so many of his colleagues on the club circuit.) Abuse from the audience came thick and fast. He attempted to increase both the pace and volume of his act in order to be heard above the increasing disorder and displeasure being freely expressed. It emerged as an exercise in personal survival, terminating in a quick exit to his Austin Mini where he felt sure he'd find his escape route home. A couple of doormen and the steward shielded him from the barrage of beer-filled miners who were determined to hound him to the door but what was clearly becoming a vicious and personal attack continued once Don was locked into his small car. Half a dozen or more of the hefty men surrounded the vehicle and began to rock it from side to side. The side wheels were quickly raised off the ground in alternate bumps, throwing Don uncontrollably around the inside of his car. The club secretary pleaded with him to get out before he was hurt but Don refused, fearing more for his life outside than in. It took several minutes and the threat of calling the police before the attack subsided and the crowd gradually dispersed but much longer before Don could bring himself to get out of the car and recover sufficiently to drive home to Birmingham.

Fortunately not all were bad experiences and others remain memorable for somewhat different reasons. In the early days of club work Don's father enjoyed accompanying his son to the different locations, often driving them to and from the venue. Occasionally they had difficulties in finding the more distant and remote clubs and on one particular occasion Don arrived with only seconds to spare. The club secretary ushered him into the makeshift dressing room at the back of the stage, instructing him to change as quickly as he could and go straight on to do his act. Charles Maclean helped his son into his stage clothes and offered to hang behind in the dressing room in order to sort out the garments that had been hastily strewn across the floor. The rather primitive facilities meant that Charles had to remain at the back of the stage throughout the performance, as his only point of exit was through the black backdrop curtain separating him from Don, who by this time was well into his routine. Unbeknown to him the next act had already arrived backstage and was preparing for her performance in yet another makeshift changing room. The audience was relaxed and responsive and Don's act was being well received but amidst the laughter he heard a 'psst, psst' sound coming from behind him. Taking a quick glance he saw his father's head poking out from behind the black curtain. The expression on his face was one of panic and horror as he whispered to Don, 'Get me out of here!' Charles Maclean's rather sheltered lifestyle had not prepared him for the brazen-ness of large female striptease artists. The lady concerned had assumed that he was part of the club management and so had naturally asked him what was expected of her that evening. The shock of an almost naked lady, as he read the situation, propositioning him, had completely disorientated Don's father, to the extent that the only thing he could think of was a quick escape via the stage. Perhaps understandably in the circumstances, he had turned to his son for help. There was little Don could do other than speed up his act. Fortunately both father and son came out of the situation unscathed but with a story that was to give them many hours of laughter in the years to come.

The clubs became the bread-and-butter work of the business. Don could always be guaranteed work and a reasonable income to tie him over in between the summer seaside and the much-loved winter pantomime seasons. Over the next three years he thrived on his performances in three different pantomimes, each one casting him appropriately as the friend of little children. The traditional elements of good fighting evil and audience participation suited Don well. Maintaining an almost constant running dialogue with the audience was never hard work for him—it came naturally, especially where children were concerned. Whether playing Buttons, Wishee Washee, Dopey Don or Idle Jack he seemed to be able to win the hearts of the youngsters; his boundless energy and natural boyish charm wooed them.

Don soon became in demand for pantomime, gaining a reputation as one of the few performers around who could gain instant contact with his audience. Small children generally have no concern for a performer's status or reputation, consequently Don knew that each time he went out on stage he started with a clean sheet. The children would either like or dislike him. He was determined to be liked and succeeded. His character was often that of the underdog, the butt of others' jokes, laughed at, teased and sometimes ignored. Frequently children identified with those feelings, freely offering their sympathy and support from their seats. Don remembers one particular moment as Buttons in *Cinderella*, when he stood alone at the front of the stage, feeling very sad that his friend Cinderella had gone off to marry Prince Charming. There was a moment of suspended silence in which all the children could sense his sadness. All of a sudden the quiet was broken by the voice of a little girl, who cried, 'Buttons, I'll marry you.' It was a poignant moment demonstrating the power of theatre and one man's skill in capturing the hearts of his audience.

Pantomime allowed Don to use everything that he could in order to make people laugh and the children were particularly responsive to the visual impact that he could create. A funny expression or silly walk, gesture or stance were quick to be seen and interpreted by the younger members of the audience. Once the children laughed the adults followed. Add to the visual a fast patter and verbal wit, plus an accomplished singing voice and you have a guaranteed recipe for success. The stage was undoubtedly his first love and he was discovering that there was nowhere better than pantomime in which he could display all his natural abilities.

Don covered considerable ground in the first few years of his professional working life and became increasingly popular with agents and booking secretaries up and down the country. Many were disappointed to hear that he had very often been booked a year or more in advance for long stints of seasonal work but each season offered greater exposure for this rising star. Felixtowe's Music Hall in the summer of 1966 became a particularly significant booking for more than one reason. It wasn't a large or particularly prestigious theatre but Don had been brought in as principal comic and for the first time in his career, featured as 'star' of the show. He quickly established a rapport with the locals and attracted unusually large numbers of youngsters from nearby Ipswich. The youth following had a great impact on Don, as it was the first time he had ever really experienced fans of his own. His confidence rose and with it an even greater determination to capture the affections of his audience. He was young, single and ambitious, the world was his oyster. He thrived on the success and even now regards that particular season as one of the most memorable of his career. In hindsight he recognizes that it marked the end of an era as the welcome responsibilities of marriage and family life that followed shortly after brought with them considerable changes in lifestyle. Don and his fans spent many enjoyable evenings together and they continued to visit the show right through the season.

Many of the visitors to this small seaside town came up from London. Amongst them this particular year was a bank manager who had clearly delighted in the young comedian's performance. On his return home he took the liberty of mentioning Don to one of his clients, a top London theatrical agent by the name of Morris Aza. Aza Artists was a well estab-lished agency which worked out of a small office in central London. Morris was grateful for the tip-off and wasted little time before going to see Don and subsequently signing him onto the agency books. It was a wonderful finish to the season, sealing the success that Don had relished all summer.

Offers of work in radio and TV were also starting to emerge and one successful appearance on BBC Radio's 'Take a Bow', a popular variety show for up-and-coming comedians, resulted in numbers of offers of work. With numerous requests now coming his way he was grateful for the support and services of a well-established and professional theatrical agent and it was Morris who secured the season at the West Cliff Theatre in Clacton in Bunny Baron's 'Starnite Spectacular' the following year. Bunny had also been impressed with Don's impact at Felixstowe and was eager to have him as top of the 'Starnite' bill.

This show was to give Don his first important television break. It was the summer of 1967, just five months after his marriage to Toni and the successful cabaret time in Australia. His confidence was running high and, as top of the bill, he dominated the show. 'Starnite' attracted a great deal of media attention on its pre-season tour of the South coast, not least because the average age of the entire company was just twenty-four years. It was advertised as a top company of Britain's rising stars. The press reported a show with 'the hallmark of a West End quality production, full of glamour, spectacle, music and comedy'. Don's performance was compared with those of Frankie Howerd and Stanley Holloway: a man with genuine star quality who was bound for the top. Predictions of a bright and prosperous future taking him far on the ladder of theatrical fame were made with great confidence and conviction. There were no reviews more pleasing to Don himself than those which appeared in the professional papers such as *The Stage*, who themselves were suggesting that the London Palladium might do well to consider him as a future prospect following his outstanding performance in the Clacton show. Their forecast was fuelled with optimism:

> *Don Maclean is bound for the top. He has that outgoing,*
> *warm quality which makes instant contact with audiences,*
> *the knack for projecting a song and unlimited energy.*
> *Nowhere is he funnier than in his own spot in this show.*

By the end of the Clacton season Don's reputation as a fast and furious stand-up comic was becoming well known in the business. When asked why he had adopted such a boisterous machine-gun-rate style of telling gags he confessed to not having the courage to work slowly. 'After all if you take time on a gag and it flops, you're stuck. My way, if three flop and the fourth clicks, it still sounds as if I am getting the laughs,' he told one newspaper reporter. It was a style he felt comfortable with, suiting his high-energy personality and approach to life although it consumed vast amounts of material. A ten- or fifteen-minute spot could take up to double the quantity of jokes used by other comedians of the day. There was always pressure on Don to find new material for his act and that pressure increased when he got his first major television opportunity following the success of 'Starnite'.

Don's agent had been trying for some time to secure him a TV contract and managed to persuade one of the directors of the Billy Cotton Music Hall to watch him in cabaret in Battersea, following the Clacton summer season. The Cotton Music Hall had been a big break for this particular director himself, who had his own sights set firmly on the big time so he was keen to give other ambitious youngsters the opportunity to prove themselves. This time his investment paid off. The Battersea visit resulted in an invitation for Don to appear live on the Saturday night 'Billy Cotton Music Hall' from London for a full six-minute solo spot. It turned out to be the most fruitful six minutes of Don Maclean's life up to that point.

Don remembers 11 May 1968 clearly. He was absolutely terrified. Everyone involved in the programme was supportive and encouraging, willing him to do well on his debut appearance. Billy Cotton gave the most wonderfully paternal introduction, making quite sure that everyone knew that this young performer was his personal discovery. Don went on with six minutes' worth of material that he hoped and prayed would bring instant laughs. It was the band that first fell about in response to one of the opening gags, 'I was so nervous about appearing here tonight that I threw myself on the floor this afternoon and missed!' That gave him all the encouragement he needed to carry on and the audience were quick to join in with raptures of laughter. He rounded the spot off with a few lines from Englebert Humperdink's chart-topping success, 'Lonely is the man without love.' Don was an instant hit, so much so, that within half an hour of the end of the show he was told that he would be wanted again. His second appearance came just a month or so later on 29 June, after which he was booked in advance to do a series of programmes for the following spring as a resident comedian on the show. Having been inundated with a variety of offers for stage, radio and television following his first appearance he was convinced that the spring series would provide the sustained exposure that he had been looking for. He was excited at the prospect, until the shattering and un-expected news of Billy Cotton's sudden death reached him. The world of light entertainment was in mourning. Not only had the BBC lost one of its finest television characters but Don had lost his contract. The disappointment was tremendous and he knew that he now had to make the most of the offers he had received from his first and only appearances on one of the most prominent shows on television at that time.

The most important and prestigious offers came from a range of television variety shows. The ultimate goal of up-and-coming stars in the business was to be able to host their own variety programmes as well as appear at the top theatres in the land, the London Palladium being the highest accolade of all. These were ambitions that Don had by now set himself in order to prove that he had what it takes to make it to the top. Appearances on 'The Roy Castle Show' and 'The Good Old Days' at Leeds City Varieties and 'Comedy Tonight' from London's famous home of cabaret, The Talk of the Town, fed that ambition. He was appearing regularly with many of the established big names in entertainment such as Roy Castle, Val Doonican, Roy Hudd and Billy Dainty, as well as many others such as Lenny Bennett, Jim Bowen, Ken Goodwin and Jerry Stephens who appeared to be making it to the top much faster than he. The collective exposure of appearing on these and other shows sustained the interest of producers in Don. His agent Morris Aza put out regular press releases making known exactly where he was working and available to be seen. The announcement frequently used the well-known catchphrase of a certain TV advert for baked beans stating, 'A million producers every day pick up their telephones and say, "... but where can we see him working?" ' It was the responsibility of Aza Artists to ensure that he was seen.

In between the television appearances most of his

consistent work at this time came from a contract with the Scottish company, The White Heather Club. Many could be forgiven for thinking that with the name Maclean Don was a natural extension to the all-Scottish cast who had become firm favourites north of the Border. They had also become extremely popular with the whole nation, through a recently broadcast television series. But he had not been selected for either his name or the fact that his family roots on his father's side had come from Scotland. The White Heather Club saw him as a rich source of comedy, with a natural ability to reach beyond the stage in drawing out warmth and response from an audience. It was a show packed with big personalities in both Don and compères Robin Hall and Jimmy MacGregor. The autumn tour of the Scottish show travelled far and wide and was a particularly happy, long stretch of work for Don and Toni, broken only by a successful pantomime season in *Aladdin,* after which Don rejoined the touring company for several weeks before enjoying the resident summer season at Llandudno. And it was during this period that Rachel Heather Maclean was born, her middle name carefully chosen in memory of this happy season with The White Heather Club. The reviews all over the country, from the north-east to the south coast, hailed him as the one of the most refreshing and original additions to the company for years. For many he was clearly the highlight of the show:

> *a fast-talking, energetic very funny patter man, he is quite one of the best laughter makers heard or seen for a very long time. The string of new jokes is almost unending and almost every one of them clean. This show is worth a visit for Don's performance alone.*

Don's time with the Scottish company was a busy and full schedule, interrupted just occasionally by a TV or radio appearance of which Yorkshire Television's 'Joker's Wild' was one. It regularly featured top comedians of the day, essentially as a joke-telling competition between two teams of three co-medians who do their best to interrupt each other's stories. Appearing with his old radio idol Ted Ray, the highly ex-perienced David Nixon and popular Les Dawson, Don not only held his own but produced some of the best gags of the eve-ning, proving both to himself and others that he could equal the performance of those who were considered the best and most experienced in the business. But despite this, recognition still only came in small doses. BBC Midland Regional television featured Don as the youngest of three stand-up comics who had come out of Birmingham in a documentary called 'Stand Up, Comic'. Whilst it was nice to receive the local interest and encouragement, this restricted regional documentary did little to raise the national profile that had now become his obsession. Work was plentiful and he was obviously still in demand but it became clear that he required the right breaks in television in order to secure the successful future that the media had now been predicting for a few years. A highly successful pantomime season at Bradford's Alhambra Theatre proved a valuable stepping stone along the way.

With Vince Hill as top of the bill, the company at the Alhambra enjoyed a happy and successful season together. Despite spartan living conditions, sickness in the Maclean household and some rather unusual media coverage of Don with stitches in his face as a result of an over-affectionate bite from ten-month-old Rachel, he thrived on the warm response of the Yorkshire audiences. The Alhambra was considered the most prestigious panto houses in the country outside London and people travelled far and wide to see the much acclaimed pantomime productions. Don's youth, good looks and singing ability had an exceptionally wide appeal and the fast patter humour went down well too. These qualities all contributed to his role as Idle Jack in *Dick Whittington*, earning him impressive reviews from the tough Northern theatre critics, one of whom maintained that Don's performance was, 'the funniest hard working Idle Jack I have seen in fifty years of pantomime going.' But it wasn't only the Yorkshire people and critics who were watching his performance on this occasion. Others had crossed the border from Lancashire. The highly influential producers of Blackpool's showcase theatres were also among the audience and they particularly liked the entertainment skills of Idle Jack. An invitation to appear the following summer with the well established and highly popular Barron Knights and dancer and vocalist Peter Gordeno at Blackpool's North Pier Pavilion was just the kind of opening Don had been looking for and he welcomed it with open arms.

7

Blackpool Breakthroughs

Don was under no illusions as to the huge professional challenge facing him in the 1970 summer season at Blackpool. It was another very important step in his career. Since Blackpool was commonly regarded as the shop window of the show business world among agents and producers, he knew that in order to gain recognition he had to shine brightly amidst its galaxy of stars. And there were plenty of them that year. Many had reached the top of the British scene years ago and were now well established in the international world of entertainment. Among the bill toppers were Tommy Steele, who was making a huge impact upon the American market and the Bachelors, also jet-setting around the world with tours in Australia, Hong Kong and Singapore. Josef Locke and Norman Wisdom, who had been 'discovered' nineteen years earlier in Blackpool, were also firm favourites in the business and drawing large crowds in one or other of Blackpool's five theatres. Others included Joan Turner and Winifred Atwell and the popular newcomer Mary Hopkin, who, like Don, was enjoying her first Blackpool season, at one of the other theatres.

The big names were in the powerful position of being able to choose exactly where and when they wanted to perform.

Producers such as Bernard Delfont had the unenviable task of filling five major theatres with entertainment that would sell out seats every night. It was no mean undertaking and the new talent brought in each year was an important part of the total scene. The privilege of being able to chose a venue was far from Don's mind as he started rehearsals for the North Pier Pavilion. At this stage he simply wanted a chance to prove himself and, despite the tough competition that surrounded him, he was determined to take full advantage of this valuable opportunity.

Bernard Delfont was the top man in show business at this time. He had many connections with film, TV and recording agencies and had set many rising stars on their way to the top of the entertainment world. His 'Showtime' at the North Pier Pavilion was just one of several impressive line-ups of stars that he had brought into Blackpool that year, with several established stage and television personalities amongst them as well as new talent such as Don and Mary Hopkin. With an emphasis on family entertainment the show's image was one of glamour and colour filled with song, dance and plenty of laughter. The experienced Barron Knights provided many of these ingredients in one act although much of the dancing came in the form of Peter Gordeno and his dancers.

The principal comic, Joe Church, was a household name in comedy and variety circles, with years of experience in making people laugh. He had done a lot of television work and appeared many times at the London Palladium. Don felt privileged to be working alongside him in the role of support comedian, joining in one or two of the sketches and choruses as well as having his own solo spot early in the first half of the programme. But it wasn't long before the enthusiastic newcomer was clearly stealing the show. From day one the newspaper headlines were announcing a new dynamic Delfont discovery in Don Maclean. Their only criticism was that his appearance on stage was all too short, leaving the crowds demanding more. Bernard Delfont's immediate response to the critics was to rearrange the entire programme after only three nights, placing Don higher on the bill than his senior colleague. Delighted though he was by this promotion he recalls being slightly apprehensive as to how Joe Church would react to being upstaged by a youngster. He need not have worried; this experienced and highly successful artist was positively delighted to see Don get his big chance, even though it meant him lowering his own profile in the process. It was a genuine expression of encouragement and sincerity rarely encountered in the cut-throat world of show business. The impact of this man's humility stayed with Don for a long time and he hoped that should he ever be in a similar position, he might be able to act in the same way.

Life backstage at the North Pier was a particularly happy time for all the performers. Many of them were married with young families who would frequently come into the theatre and meet up behind the scenes. Several arranged to converge daily on Blackpool's beaches, spending many happy hours together in the sunshine. When the husbands rushed back to the theatre for the early evening performance, the wives and children would remain together, offering companionship throughout the long summer away from home.

The season turned out to be the dream come true that Don had always hoped for. He was clearly the centre of attention. With critics fighting to have their praises and predictions heard and both local and national press requesting personal profile interviews Don's confidence level rose with each day. It was also a glorious summer, with a long sustained heatwave intensifying the warm feeling of success. The media attention widened beyond the immediate interest in the act to embrace the much broader personality of a man who was clearly devoted to his wife and young daughter. Toni and eighteen-month-old Rachel joined in the limelight, enjoying photographic sessions of family days on the beach. The image of the successful family entertainer was a journalist's delight and there seemed few Northern papers which didn't focus on this very real and appealing side to Blackpool's latest discovery.

In fact there was very little that Don and Toni could do that summer without it being reported in the press. They began the round of church fête and garden party openings and charity concerns, always appearing together along with Rachel. Don was never too busy to accept the invitations that came his way and was particularly pleased when he was invited to take part in a special mass for the Catholic Stage Guild at Blackpool Sacred Heart Roman Catholic Church. To take his place alongside other Catholics in the business, such as Joe Gladwin of TV's 'Nearest and Dearest' fame and Mary Ryan, a former Covent Garden performer, was a particular delight to him. A column called 'Blackpool Breezes' in one of the local newspapers also allowed him to engage in a very personal form of correspondence with holiday-makers and Don enjoyed commenting on a number of issues and events taking place in the holiday town that summer. He was never short of material or ideas, ranging from his strong anti-smoking opinions as a member of the Society of Non-Smokers (joining the likes of Cliff Richard, Ken Dodd, Brian Rix and Norman Vaughan) to sharing little snippets of personal information about other performers and shows working in the Blackpool scene that summer. It became clear that Don's writing skills were not restricted to a string of gags and humorous sketches.

Throughout the enormously successful season at Blackpool the question of what would follow after was always at the back of his mind. The critics' accolades only really meant something if and when they were translated into concrete offers of work. Prophetic words from journalists were all very exciting to read but still needed to become a reality.

Billy Marsh was one of the most influential people in the business, working very closely with Mr Delfont. When he spoke, people listened and he chose the end of the Blackpool season in which to make several confident predictions in the world of comedy entertainment. He had been around for some time, his observations were sharp and accurate and he was recognizing the very different routes that were now producing the then current 'new wave' of entertainers. The last big stream of talent in the comedy world had emerged after World War II. People such as Frankie Howerd, Max Bygraves, Harry Secombe and Peter Sellers had learned their trade from entertaining the troops and then emerged in the old music halls around the country. They then branched out into radio, the medium through which Don had encountered them and later, television.

Billy Marsh was quick to acknowledge that the current generation had worked their way up through clubs and holiday camps and were now looking desperately for the exposure needed to launch a career. Television was the obvious vehicle but an ambitious entertainer needed to be noticed in order to get a television opportunity. Don, in Billy Marsh's opinion, was one of the youngsters who deserved that chance and he confidently forecast a place for him at the London Palladium before the year was out. Other names listed in Billy Marsh's predictions at this time included Larry Grayson, Norman Collier—who had been working many of the same club circuits as Don—and the lesser-known Peter Hudson and Bobby Knoxall.

Don was delighted to be noticed by one of the most powerful experts in the business and very quick to accept the advice and opportunities that came his way. *The Stage* newspaper maintained that with the expertise of Aza Artists, the interest of London-based Marsh and being on the Delfont payroll, professionally speaking his ultimate 'arrival' was merely a matter of time. There was little doubt that the North Pier's 'Showtime' had done more to underline his potential as a future star than all the experience of the last six years put together.

A journalist from *The Observer* newspaper chose that particular summer in which to write a centre-page feature article about British seaside entertainment. His research was thorough; he had clearly spent days, if not weeks, watching numerous performers and performances. His comments about the North Pier Theatre and in particular Don's part in the show rather dominated the article and attracted great interest in London, sending several agents and producers North in search of a star. Ronald Bryden claimed:

> *the hit of the evening is Don Maclean, a dark-haired wicked young comedian who works like a high-speed welder, showering acid one-liner gags over the audience almost too fast for laughs... the skill and pace are hard to resist and the material's all fresh. He's cheered like an outrageous nephew at a family wedding, the one in the sharp suit.*

Amongst the London visitors were the influential Palladium scouts who were quick to fulfil the prophecies by offering Don his much longed-for invitation to appear at London's premier theatre just two months later, in November 1970. Newspaper headlines announced 'Don's call to the big time'. He joined a cast of five for a two-hour variety-packed show. Top of the bill was Englebert Humperdinck, who started his performing life in the clubs as Gerry Dorsey but had since risen to the dizzy heights of stardom with a reputation as the world's most romantic singer. The Dallas Boys were invited to open the show, providing a sharp, crisp act of songs and comedy impressions, leaving Don and finally Clodagh Rogers to complete the first half. Englebert filled the second half himself. Don's act lasted twelve minutes and he had two weeks in which to pack in as much original material as he could. Nobody was more supportive of the challenge than journalists from his own Birmingham who surrounded him with words of encouragement and confidence and cries of 'we always knew you'd make it to the top, Don.' He needed all the encouragement he could get for he knew that this performance was the highest springboard that the profession could offer and he intended to use it well.

The first night brought back memories of his nerve-racking appearance on the 'Billy Cotton Music Hall' show. He could hardly believe that he was going to step out onto the same stage where international stars like Jerry Lewis and Judy Garland had performed. He became even more tense when told that the opening night had four huge names in show business sitting on the very front row. Englebert Humperdinck was an enormously popular performer of the day and it was a common practice for one's peers in the world of entertainment to be invited guests to first-night performances. Leslie Grade, Tom Jones, Des O'Connor and Raquel Welch were amongst the select few in Don's direct line of gaze, underlining for him the importance of his impact at this prestigious theatre. He was still very young—twenty-six years of age—and desperate to meet the expectations of those who had given him this wonderful opportunity.

In hindsight Don realizes that his desperation on this occasion was a little too great. The show's producers had managed to persuade him that the London audiences would be very different to those he had experienced in Blackpool and had suggested that he made his act a touch more sophisticated and fitting for a more professional clientele. Eric Davidson, Don's writer at that time, had written new material for him and he spent the preceding weeks familiarizing himself with it in the hope that it would achieve what was necessary. Sadly on that opening night, it didn't. The material was cold and Don knew he hadn't used it enough to feel completely relaxed in his delivery. It was a long way from the success he had experienced in the North. Whilst there had been some response it was far from the hysterical paralysis that he had caused night after night at Blackpool's North Pier. He came off the stage bitterly disappointed and, instead of celebrating the phenomenal success that he had hoped for, set about the task of re-writing his material for the following night. It took him a week to find the confidence to return to the act that he knew people had loved but, by the end of the fortnight, he was getting the over-whelming audience response that had become so familiar. Despite his initial fears and inner struggle the critics' reviews were positive and encouraging, announcing him as 'the best new comic since Jimmy Tarbuck' and further offers of work came steadily his way. One article described him on stage as

> *a clip-syllabled maelstrom, spitting out jokes with the urgency of a firecracker at full throttle. Eyes that round with mock alarm; arms that fling his every gesture to the outer limits of expansiveness; a mouth that splits into a gash of strong-toothed mischief.*

During the two weeks at the Palladium Don and Toni had stayed with her parents in their flat in Pimlico. Tom Roux, Toni's father, had accompanied Don every day to the theatre, helping him to get ready and entertaining friends and family backstage in his dressing room. He loved every single minute of his time spent there. At the end of each evening he was reluctant to go home, having soaked up the atmosphere and revelled in the glory and success of his son-in-law. As their time came to an end both men savoured the moments together, enjoying a very special friendship and a joint passion for the magic of one of London's greatest theatre. On the last night Don clearly remembers sitting up in bed, not wanting to sleep because he didn't want the Palladium experience to end.

The autumn and winter period following the Blackpool season was extremely busy. Apart from the Palladium fortnight, numerous invitations to do spots on TV variety shows had continued to come Don's way. Most of them were pre-recorded, involving him in hours of rehearsals and filming. Two in particular were prime-time shows, hosted by Jimmy Tarbuck and Leslie Crowther, both of whom had already made their mark in the world of entertainment. Don's popularity among the Scots also continued as he became a much-loved guest on BBC Scotland's 'Lena Martell Show'. Two television opportunities of a different kind came in the shape of a regional revue-type show called 'Seventy in the Shade' and a quiz show, 'Out for the Count'. Both gave Don more scope for using the full breadth of his personality and the ability to handle people in quite different situations. Previously he had only ever appeared as a guest on quiz shows, so he welcomed this opportunity to host and act as referee. Alongside his regular variety act performances it was a challenge, stretching and developing his skills, especially his ability to ad lib when required.

'Out for the Count' replaced a Tuesday evening slot normally occupied by the popular programme 'Contact'. Based on the rules of boxing—with punches replaced by questions—it challenged inter-county teams to answer questions on general knowledge. It ran for six weeks and, even though it was screened late in the evening, succeeded in attracting over one million viewers by the time it reached the final. Don was delighted with the success and knew full well that if the BBC decided to network it nationally it could reach an audience of over seven million people. This, he hoped, might well become the national television programme that would sustain and secure his profile as one of the country's top performers.

Most of the work during this period took place on home ground in Birmingham, or in London, where the family were able to stay with Toni's parents. It was only when the pantomime season began in Oxford that they once more made their home in rented accommodation. It was a happy season, working with Jimmy Edwards and Peter Glaze in *Sleeping Beauty* and Don delighted audiences and critics alike in his side-splitting role as the court jester. But beyond the jokes he was clearly being recognized as the one performer who had both the ability and the power of personality to create an atmosphere of happiness within the theatre. He set out with the intention of befriending the audience and in return expected them to befriend him. And as far as the critics were concerned he succeeded every time.

The period between the Blackpool summer season and Oxford pantomime had been relentless. Numerous television appearances interspersed with successful cabaret, pantomime and theatre work had kept Don working week after week and sustained the interest of the media. But he was still waiting for the guarantee of a television series in order to secure his reputation in the business as one of the top artists around. His hopes were fixed on 'Out for the Count' but in the spring of 1971 he finally heard that the BBC had decided not to repeat the highly popular and successful quiz show. It came as a great disappointment to him and he failed to hide his reaction from the media. Around the same time his agent also told him that negotiations for Don to spend the summer season in the 'Norman Wisdom Show' at Great Yarmouth had also fallen through. It was a bitter double blow, at a time when his hopes had been raised and he had felt confident that he had a chance of breaking through into the big time. For the first time ever in his professional career, which had now spanned some seven years, he was momentarily attracted by the possibility of living elsewhere. The opportunity came his way quite unexpectedly.

Only seconds after coming off stage at a Sunday night performance at London's Victoria Palace a knock came at Don's dressing-room door. The accent was Australian and the request quite direct. 'Would you like a season's work at the St George's Leagues Club in Sydney?' The agent, Bryan Fehon, was under strict instructions to find a British comedian to star in a show called 'Tokyo by Night' and send him out to Sydney as soon as possible. The offer was tempting for Don and Toni; it brought back fond memories of their honeymoon and the highly successful cabaret appearances a few years earlier. The thought of taking Rachel back with them to meet both Toni's sister and family as well as friends and acquaintances from the last trip was a strong pull they eventually couldn't resist. Once the news of Great Yarmouth had filtered through the network, other offers of summer seasons came in but Don decided to take the risk forsaking a British summer for a cabaret tour of New South Wales, Australia. Within a week they were packed and on their way to Sydney.

The show broke all box office records at the mammoth St George's Leagues Club and he was inundated with offers to remain in Australia. But one very important reason drew him back to England. For the very first time Don was offered a season's work in his home town of Birmingham, starring alongside the Bachelors and Frank Carson in *Jack and the Beanstalk*. It had been something he had always wanted and it provided the incentive to return home. The thought of a Christmas in their family home in Selly Oak was equally appealing.

Performing at home presented numerous opportunities for interviews and media interest generally and the Birmingham debut turned out to be an all-time box-office success. As far as the locals were concerned, Don was top of the bill. The press were unanimous in their praise of his performance and audiences loved his own particular brand of quick-fire humour and especially his Birmingham accent. The city was also sympathetic towards his frustrations and he found a very supportive platform on which to voice his feelings sensitively about his lack of recognition in the country. It seemed that everyone in the business had worked with him and knew him but trying to establish himself as a national household name was proving extremely difficult. It was becoming a slow process of chipping away at an enormous block. Finding work wasn't the problem— he was still being inundated with offers, including one or two very high-profile appearances following in the footsteps of people such as Bob Monkhouse and Leslie Crowther. Radio also made its demands, as Don found himself once more developing his skills in script-writing for a Radio 4 programme called

'Regional Extraordinary'. The frustrations were alleviated slightly when he learned that he had been offered another season in Blackpool at the more prestigious Opera House Theatre, starring with Cilla Black. This, combined with the fact that his and Toni's second child was due just two days before that season was due to start, helped him to look a little more optimistically at the immediate future.

Rory Gregor Maclean's arrival into the world was perfectly timed, just four days before the opening night of his father's summer season. Don had secretly hoped he would be on time, simply so that his first-night nerves might be relieved of the potential anxiety of having a wife in labour. As it happened, he had four days in which to get used to being a father of two although very little time to get to know his son as he was busy rehearsing up in Blackpool. The news that Toni had gone into labour reached him soon enough to make the journey back to Birmingham to be present at the birth but, just as had been the case with Rachel, it was a case of a quick cuddle and back to work. But the separation wasn't for long; it was only a week or two before Toni and the children were joining him in their rented Blackpool accommodation.

Eight weeks later the extended family travelled North for Rory's christening at the Sacred Heart Church, Talbot Square. Father Paul Chamberlain, a close friend of Don's since St Philip's Grammar School days, also made the journey, in order to complete the family occasion by officiating at the ceremony. However, Rory's godparents didn't have to travel far at all, as they were already in their seasonal residence in Blackpool. Fellow comedian Frank Carson and his wife Ruth had become close friends of the Macleans and were delighted to take on the responsibility of being godparents to Don's new-born son. Once more the Northern press delighted in covering every aspect of this young, happy family's life. And the reviews of the 'Opera House International Spectacular '72' were equally complimentary. He was as delighted to be back in Blackpool as Blackpool was delighted to have him. The combination of the person-alities of Cilla, fellow Scouser Johnny Hackett and Don was a guaranteed success and the Opera House enjoyed packed houses nearly all through the season. Don was first on stage and carried the huge responsibility of warming the audience up. Once more, his natural ability to reach out beyond the stage came to the forefront and did not go unnoticed by a group of London producers who were on the lookout for someone to host a top London-based show the following spring.

Blackpool had once again raised his profile in the country and stirred the interest of different agents. He had six months of top cabaret work to look forward to in the Showboat Theatre Restaurant in London's Trafalgar Square, as well as a weekly appearance on BBC's 'Pebble Mill At One' lunchtime magazine programme. It was this short comedy spot, when Don was acting as the 'Raving' Reporter, that led to a most unexpected opportunity to work on the country's leading children's programme of the time.

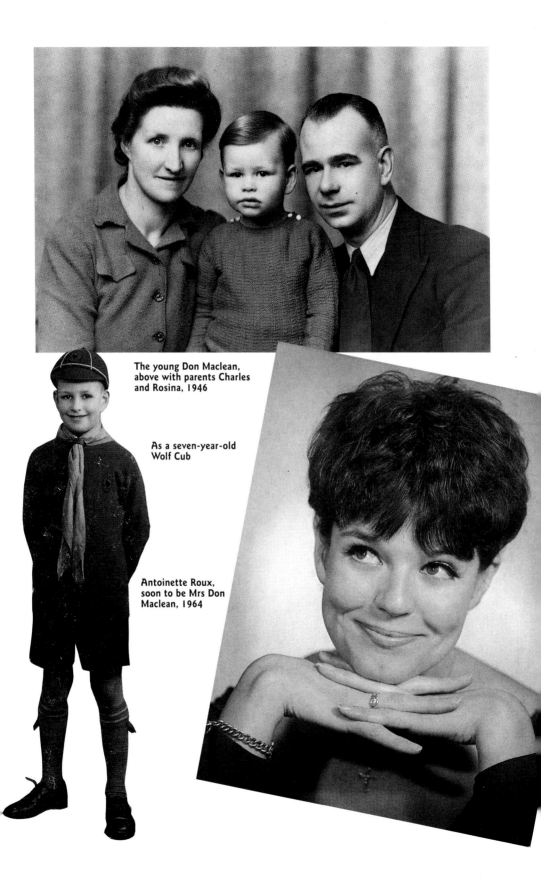

The young Don Maclean, above with parents Charles and Rosina, 1946

As a seven-year-old Wolf Cub

Antoinette Roux, soon to be Mrs Don Maclean, 1964

Don's first
publicity photo,
1964

Wedding day,
11 February 1967

ABOVE: **Performing with long-time friend Frank Carson, 1973** (Shirley M. Hill)

LEFT: **Don in BBC TV's 'The Good Old Days', 1969** (Barry Wilkinson)

BELOW: **As many will remember Don with Peter Glaze in 'Crackerjack', 1975** (Ron Howard)

ABOVE: With Pam Ayres in BBC TV's 'Black and White Minstrel Show', 1976 (Radio Times)

ABOVE RIGHT: Performing with Cilla Black in her Bournemouth show, 1979

As star of his own enormously popular radio comedy show of the early eighties

With Les Dawson in *Babes in the Wood*, 1981

ABOVE: Entertaining the troops, Port Stanley, Falklands Islands, 1983

LEFT: With Joe Black and Bob Grant in the Rogers & Hammerstein musical of *Cinderella*, at the Birmingham Repertory Theatre, 1982. Don is Buttons! (Mel Figures)

With Mandy Rice-Davies, 1984
(Mel Figures)

**Radio 2's 'Press Gang'
team, 1989**
(BBC)

'The Cheapest Show on Telly' featured the young Lenny Henry, 1979 (Mel Figures)

ABOVE: Radio 2's 'Good Morning Sunday' with Cannon and Ball in 1993

BELOW: David Smith cartoon of Don and the British Celebrity Squash Team, 1980. From top left, clockwise: Don Maclean, William Franklin, Leonard Rossiter, Tommy Steele, John Cleese, James Hunt, Jasper Carrott

Easter Day 1995, when Don recorded a special edition of 'Good Morning Sunday' from Vatican Square

LEFT: **Don with Archbishop Desmond Tutu on 'Good Morning Sunday', 1994** (BBC)

Proud father Don with son Rory and daughter Rachel, 1990

(left, Birmingham Post and Mail, right, Mel Figures)

8
Prime-Time Television

Picture the scene. It's Colditz Castle. Two British officers, cunningly disguised as Michael Aspel and Peter Glaze, are conferring about their escape.

'Tonight,' says Glaze, 'we must get out tonight.'

'No, not tonight,' says Aspel.

'Why not?'

'Because it's Friday night... it's five to five... it's "Crackerjack",' says Aspel, as a German soldier sticks a bayonet in his backside.

A loud screaming chorus of 'Crackerjack' reverberates around a London television studio from the hundreds of children packed in and is further echoed around the nation by millions more glued to their television screens.

The popular children's programme of the late fifties, sixties and seventies had become a British institution, providing thirteen weeks a year of high-energy entertainment. It also became a springboard for many an ambitious entertainer looking for a higher profile in the world of television. On this occasion the German soldier was Don Maclean, the latest in a talented line of celebrated showbusiness personalities to land himself with the coveted comedy spot on the BBC's then most successful children's television series. His multi-talented skills gave 'Crackerjack' the new lease of life that the programme's makers had been looking for. It was an unexpected invitation to join co-presenters Peter Glaze, Michael Aspel and later Ed Stewart, which came, surprisingly, through his appearances on an adult show.

As part of the official opening of the Pebble Mill television studios in Birmingham in the autumn of 1972 the BBC approached Don about scripting and appearing in a short comedy spot that would become part of a pilot programme called 'Pebble Mill At One'. It was an unusual invitation coming from a magazine-type programme presented largely by journalists. His name had cropped up because the same group of people had put together the regional documentary 'Stand Up, Comic', in which Don had featured, a few years earlier. When the request came he was still working the summer season at Blackpool's Opera House but agreed to write and make a programme of some eight minutes. It featured himself as the Galloping Gardener whom he describes as an irreverent cross between Graham Kerr (known as the Galloping Gourmet) and Percy Thrower, television's well-known gardener. It was both a challenge and an experiment in using comedy in quite a different way to the conventional stand-up role that he was used to.

Don was convinced that comedy on television had to change. Over the previous few years the stand-up comedian had received massive exposure through the popular series 'The Comedians'. It consumed vast amounts of material and severely restricted—some say, even killed off—the future use of the traditional stand-up comic on the small screen. Don felt sure that television could provide a number of other ways of portraying humour, not least in using the medium's technical tricks to the full. The pilot programme was a success and led to the commissioning of a series for 'Pebble Mill At One'. As part of that deal Don was offered a twelve-week contract to make twelve further films for the autumn series. It was simply a short comedy spot in which he became known as the show's Raving Reporter. Each week he would present a humorous sketch based on a wide range of topics from different locations. Some of the twelve films were shot as outside broadcasts during his Blackpool season, making the most of local features such as the trams and beaches. 'Maclean's Olympics' and 'The Great Tram Robbery' were just two of the twelve to be screened each Friday during the autumn months.

Whilst the opportunity was good experience and he enjoyed the challenge of bringing comedy into the programme in a new and refreshing way, it also had its frustrations. He remembers wanting to do a sketch involving a set of woolly combinations—on that occasion the wardrobe department couldn't accommodate him and he had to go out and buy his own! The Birmingham studios didn't really have the facilities for the type of comedy Don was trying to introduce but the slot proved to be a vital stepping stone to bigger things. The actual timing of the Raving Reporter on 'Pebble Mill' was highly significant as it coincided with children coming home from school during their lunch break. They lapped up his quick-witted humour and wanted more. Being screened around that time during the tea-time children's TV slot was a programme called 'Ask Aspel' (presented by Michael Aspel), which invited youngsters to write in and request their favourite parts of programmes to be repeated. The Raving Reporter of 'Pebble Mill At One' was requested time and time again. Don had obviously struck a chord somewhere with the youngsters. It was following these numerous requests that the BBC began to wonder if Don might well be the one to bring back to life the flagging 'Crackerjack'. When the offer came his way he was quick to accept, realizing the potential of appearing on a prime-time weekly children's show.

'Crackerjack' had been running since the mid-fifties, launching personalities such as Leslie Crowther, Ronnie Corbett and Eamonn Andrews, all of whom had achieved phenomenal success through the show. The decision to finish it completely would have been the end of an era but the previous series had gone through difficult times with viewing figures taking a noticeable drop and it was an option the BBC were seriously considering until Don's talents were brought to their attention. In inviting him to join the team they decided to give it one more go, in the hope that their new comedy team member would breathe new life into the show. (Michael Aspel clearly remembers Don joining the team, not least because of his insistence that they all pronounced his name correctly. The American singer Don McLean had enjoyed tremendous popularity in England around this time with his hit single 'American Pie' and the two men were frequently confused despite the fact that their names were pronounced quite differently. On one occasion Don even had a coach full of girls turn up to one of his shows thinking they had booked to see the singer, not the comedian!)

Don never deliberately set out to entertain children and he was always pleased that 'Crackerjack' was produced by the BBC's light entertainment department as opposed to the makers of specifically children's programmes. The teatime slot was simply 'borrowed' from Monica Simms, the then Head of Children's Television. Of course, having children in his audience wasn't a completely new experience, since he had worked as a family entertainer both in pantomime and summer seasons but having to hold the attention of a child-only clientele was a challenge that he took very seriously. As far as he could see there wasn't a clearly defined 'child' humour. Children loved the adult light entertainment of the day, such as 'Dad's Army', 'Morecambe and Wise' and 'The Two Ronnies'. The key, to his mind, was to bring the humour within the boundaries of their experiences but not to run the risk of patronizing them as he felt so many children's entertainers of the day did. His theory succeeded in practice. In the first series viewing figures rose rapidly and school groups fought to get studio tickets. This, in turn, led to fierce competition from pop groups of the day wanting a live spot on the show, fully realizing the record-selling potential of such an appearance. Not surprisingly the first led to a further three series, with statistics showing peak viewing times drawing more than 8.5 million people, over half of whom were adults. Don thrived on nearly five years of working for the BBC on 'Crackerjack', between 1972 and 1977.

It was a gruelling schedule, filling almost six of the seven days in the week, made all the more difficult for Don during the first series because he was working every night at the Showboat Theatre Restaurant in cabaret. The 'Crackerjack' week began on Wednesdays when the team met to talk through the following week's programme. Thursdays would be spent filming outside, followed by Fridays and at least Saturday mornings rehearsing. Sunday was a welcome day off. Monday morning was a technical run-through followed by a reading of the following week's show in the afternoon. The team then spent all day Tuesday in the theatre rehearsing until the evening, when hundreds of children appeared for the actual live filming, after which the cycle would begin again. Unless there was a major disaster very little editing of the programme took place and it eventually went out three days later, on the Friday, at five to five.

There was a very definite structure to the programme, the elements of which suited Don's personality perfectly. Musical items, audience participation, zany sketches, team games involving the children all played their parts but none more so than the silent movie slots. He formed an effective and close working relationship with Peter Glaze. It wasn't the first time that they had enjoyed a successful partnership, having teamed up in pantomime both in Oxford and Birmingham's Hippodrome only a year or two earlier. Peter was somewhat of an institution on 'Crackerjack'. He was the one team member who had remained during several changes. The revival of the silent movie spot emerged as a result of the two men's discovery of a joint love of slapstick comedy. It wasn't entirely new to the show although it hadn't been featured since Leslie Crowther had left several years earlier. Don and Peter thrived on its resurrection.

Don often thought he had been born into the wrong era, feeling sure that he would have been very much more suited to the Laurel and Hardy generation of film-making. At first the producers were wary about its reinstatement in the show, fearing high costs of production and extended hours of filming but when Don and Peter formed their own independent film company, taking on the total responsibility of making such scenes, the BBC were quick to be first in the queue to buy them for 'Crackerjack'. They were all based on silent visual humour, aimed at fitting in at least a dozen laughs into five minutes of film.

As two characters they fell comfortably into two definite roles. Both were quite idiotic but one thought he was more intelligent than the other. Most of the humour was based on Don pricking Peter Glaze's pomposity and it worked. Other television companies from various European countries were showing interest in viewing the films and at one stage they even had inquiries from China. The BBC also screened them as films in their own right, apart from 'Crackerjack' and they proved extremely popular with schoolchildren during their holiday period. But the most prestigious showing of all came when the BBC decided to enter some of the films for the Cannes Film Festival. Nobody was more surprised than Don but it confirmed his conviction of the international and eternal appeal of the silent movie.

This double act received many accolades over the five years the two men worked together, frequently being compared with the skill and wit of Morecambe and Wise but the greatest compliment of all, in Don's mind, came in a *Daily Mail* article during the mid-seventies' three-day week employment difficulties. The journalist concerned encouraged the British workforce with the thought that one very positive outcome of the shortened working week was that everyone could now arrive home in time to see Maclean and Glaze on Friday's episode of 'Crackerjack'! Don carried the cutting in his wallet for many years.

Making the silent movies and filming other sketches for 'Crackerjack' had its down side too, proving, at times, extremely hazardous for Don. Many artists would have employed the skills of a stunt man to stand in for them but Don remained convinced that children were amongst the most perceptive of audiences and would spot a substitute within seconds. He had no intention of trying to fool them and so took on the daring and demanding acts of physical challenge himself. But there were times when even the simplest of everyday activities left him battered, bruised and bandaged and at one stage the ever-increasing catalogue of disasters began to worry the BBC. In filming just one series he was badly bitten by a dog; fell off a stepladder on the back of a moving truck (five stitches to a face wound); jumped off a moving jeep, over a 2m (6ft) hedge and into a pond (heavy bruising and grazes); slid down the roof of a circus tent and fell off the edge, missing the safety net (unable to sit down for several days); been towed behind a speedboat on his stomach (bruised ribs); and hoisted 20m (60ft) up a church belltower (temporary deafness from getting too close to the bell).

On a more serious note, he was once filming on location in central London, playing the part of an accident-prone fireman. The idea was for Don to be transported up the front of the building on the jet of water from his hose. This was to be achieved by using a hidden crane and a winch wire around his waist. However something went wrong and the machinery operated too fast. Don rocketed up, struck his head on a windowledge and plummeted 5m (16ft) to the pavement below. Fortunately he was wearing a safety helmet but his back and spine were hurt and he had to spend several weeks in a surgical collar. After that particular accident the BBC did employ a stunt man, leaving him to shoot the simpler tasks, such as peeling onions. Even then he succeeded in cutting his finger with the razor-sharp chopping knife and holding up filming for an hour whilst they tried to stop the bleeding! The media had a field day on the star who became known as the most accident-prone in the business.

Four series of 'Crackerjack' brought with them a lot of work and positive media attention, all of which raised Don's profile in the entertainment world. Neither were his appearances for the programme restricted to Friday nights at five to five. Special editions for Bank Holiday or Christmas viewing were also slotted into the schedule, especially when it came to the choice of Christmas pantomime on television. For two consecutive years the BBC brought in the entire 'Crackerjack' cast to entertain the nation. Don thoroughly enjoyed the experience of doing pantomime in a studio instead of a theatre, taking full advantage of the technical effects in order to bring an even greater magic into the show. During this time his popularity with children also attracted a wide range of hospital, school and children's charitable engagements which Don made every effort to fulfil. There was rarely a day during this period when he could go out of his house without hearing, somewhere in the distance, the rousing cry of someone shouting 'Crackerjack!'

One of the most privileged invitations to come his way, as a direct result of 'Crackerjack' and an indication of the impact that he was having in the entertainment world, was the opportunity to host and present a Spring Bank Holiday Disneytime special. He was following in a long line of well-known and popular personalities from the worlds of sport, music, screen and stage. Only weeks before, racing-car driver Graham Hill had sat in the honoured presenter's seat, following earlier stars such as Paul and Linda McCartney, Cilla Black and Rolf Harris. Don was flattered to be selected as presenter for what was recognized as prestige holiday viewing time and delighted also to share the job with his friend and partner Peter Glaze. Together they set themselves the ambitious challenge of doing the show from an old cinema, creating an atmosphere of set and screen into which they drew their captive audience. Two of the most delighted youngsters to watch were his own children, Rachel and Rory, who had become compulsive viewers of anything that their daddy was doing on television.

The only disadvantage of working on 'Crackerjack' for such a long period of time was that it all took place in London. As the first series clashed with cabaret the daytime was spent rehearsing and filming the programme and evenings as top of the bill at London's Showboat Theatre Restaurant. It was an exhausting time and one of the longest periods Don had spent away from his native Birmingham, something he always vowed he'd avoid at all costs. It wasn't long before the family decided to rent a house in Twickenham, in order to be together but when yet another plum London-based job came Don's way it became clear that they would have to rethink their hard and fast decision never to move out of their home city. The outcome was a compromise: they decided to purchase a second house in London, as a permanent base for those times both then and in the future when Don needed to work there. It offered Toni and the children familiarity and stability during one of the busiest periods of Don's working life but never replaced their real home in much-loved Birmingham.

Among the many London-based producers who had travelled up to Blackpool's Opera House to see Don at work were Robert Luff, George Mitchell and Ernest Maxim who were responsible for the new stage production of the internationally famous Black and White Minstrels. They had been impressed with this comedian's ability to hold an audience in a vast theatre with 3,000 seats, especially at the start of the show and it was precisely these skills they were looking for. The Minstrels' stage show had been running for some years, first launched in 1960 by Robert Luff but was short-lived due to considerable financial loss. It reopened two years later and became a showbusiness phenomenon. Running for seven years non-stop, it played to an audience of almost five million people. Eleven years after its original conception, it still remained a strong feature of the London entertainment scene, as well as reaping enthusiastic audiences in the provinces with its touring companies.

The Black and Whites acquired an international reputation and Don's selection as the resident comedian was a true accolade, singling him out as one of the country's top entertainers. He was particularly pleased to be chosen as, five years earlier in 1967, when appearing in the highly successful 'Starnite' show at Clacton, the producers of the Black and Whites had been to watch him several times with a view to offering him the job then. It would have been a tremendous break so early on in his career but never came off at that stage. His disappointment then had been great but to have been successfully reconsidered some years later truly delighted him. Even he was beginning to believe that his turn for the big time had finally arrived. 'Crackerjack' had made him a household name but he was beginning to fear that people would categorize him as a children's entertainer. Now he was gaining recognition with people in the business who had never watched 'Crackerjack'.

The opening night at the New Victoria Theatre in July 1973 brought rave reviews, heralding him as one of the best comedy inputs the show had ever known. One national paper maintained he had stolen the show, declaring:

One man scores what must be the biggest ever personal success in what is essentially a team effort. Don Maclean collected the only encore of the evening and had he been allowed a solo entrance in the finale the odds are that he would have roused a louder response than the Minstrels themselves.

Combining 'Crackerjack' with the Black and Whites proved quite challenging. On more than one occasion Don went on to the New Victoria Theatre with one or other of his 'Crackerjack' injuries clearly visible to the audience, frequently integrating his wounds successfully into his act. The night of the bomb scare proved particularly hilarious. With just minutes before the curtain was due to go up, the entire theatre had to be vacated, due to a phone call informing the management that a bomb had been planted in the auditorium. Don joined the crowds in the side streets of the theatre. Fortunately the incident was a hoax but naturally the show was late starting and the audience was a little unsettled by the inconvenience of having to leave the auditorium. As soon as Don had re-entered the theatre he was instructed to go on stage and talk to the audience as they found their seats for the second time that evening. Both arms were bandaged, one bandage extending up to his fingertips, he was limping quite badly and had cuts and bruises all over his face. Taking full advantage of the captive audience he hobbled pathetically onto the stage clutching a microphone. 'Ladies and gentlemen,' he announced, 'I found the bomb!' Don's timing was perfect in every way. Not only did it produce the biggest laugh of the night; it defused a potentially tense situation, relaxing audience and artists and allowing them to go on to enjoy a good evening's entertainment.

Don was clearly one of the big names on the London entertainment scene whilst appearing at the New Victoria. Another was Bruce Forsyth who was doing a series of Saturday nights at the London Palladium. One particular week during August Bruce was struck down with every entertainer's nightmare of a complaint—a loss of voice. With just an hour's notice Don was called upon to take his place. He rushed over to the Palladium, handled the first half of the show and dashed back to the New Victoria in time to appear in the second half of the Black and Whites. Ronnie Corbett took over for him during the Palladium's second half and the whole process was repeated for a second night. It was yet another accolade singling Don out as one of the country's top performers.

The seven-month London season led to the first of several happy summer seasons with the company at venues such as Paignton, Bournemouth, Scarborough and yet another welcome return to Blackpool in 1976. The workload was so great by this time that Don was very much in need of the skills of a professional writer who could turn out vast quantities of good topical, up-to-date material for his long summer season stretches. Howard Imber became that man. They met through Don's guest appearance on 'The Golden Shot' at the invitation of Bob Monkhouse and struck up an immediate friendship. Howard was then writing topical jokes for BBC Radio 4's 'Week Ending' programme and sent Don samples of his material. It became the start of a friendship and working relationship that was to continue for many years.

Howard remembers their early days together with the Black and Whites with great affection. The two men were of a similar age and shared common experiences and recollections from their early childhood. Much of the material that Howard wrote during that time was based on their nostalgic memories of those years. The audiences loved Don's flamboyant, detailed description of arriving home from school on Mondays to find the house filled with a fog from the steam of wash day, so much so that when the budgie jumped from one perch to the next, he missed! His nightly patter about woolly bathing costumes, knotted handkerchief sunhats and ladies' suspenders struck a nostalgic chord in his audiences too, producing hours of laughter night after night. He was always keen to get plenty of local knowledge integrated into his act, especially when on summer seasons. If a place had strong local characteristics, he would make good use of them, feeding Howard with the facts and waiting for the goods to be produced. There were some weeks when the two men would be on the phone daily, exchanging information and updating material so that it was fresh, new and topical. The 1977 summer season in Scarborough became a particularly successful time, with the press loving the energy put into the act. One local newspaper described in detail Don's performance at the Futurist Theatre, highlighting his effort to make use of the unusual North East foggy summer days known as 'sea frets':

> *Striding purposefully up the centre aisle, he thrusts the microphone into the bemused face of Olive from Middlesborough, end of the tenth-row whist drive party. "Allo Olive.' Appreciative shrieks from her friends. 'What about these sea frets? Only seaside resort where the donkeys are fitted with fog lamps.'*

Many of Don's predecessors in the Black and Whites had produced a number of comedy spots that were dropped into the show at appropriate points, often talking at the audience. He tried hard to move away from that detached and distant format and made a distinct effort to integrate comedy into the whole show, linking together all the different factions in as humorous a way as possible. Don's unique ability to befriend an audience and create a family atmosphere inside a theatre frequently resulted in them eating from the palms of his hands. *The Stage*'s report of one particular summer season read:

> *The show's guest star is Don Maclean who, suitably, makes his entrance seemingly rocket propelled. And this first entrance earns for him as much applause as would satisfy any bill topper taking his final curtain.*

Success with the Minstrels went from strength to strength. In 1975, two years after the start of the London stage production, Don clinched a major signing for the BBC 'Black and White Minstrels' television series. At first he was invited to do a Christmas special, the success of which led to a series of six shows at the peak viewing time of 8.15p.m. on a Saturday night. Once more working with Howard Imber and also with Tony Hare, his new material and ideas displayed a unique style of comedy performance. They introduced hysterically funny scenes featuring several BBC 'backroom' characters such as Gideon Goodbody, a dress designer, Blodwyn Leeks the tea lady and Cyril Cutback, the ruthless man in charge of finance. It won approval from viewers and critics alike, with audience figures reaching phenomenally high viewing statistics. The show's producer, Ernest Maxim, was quite confident in staking his reputation on Don becoming a permanent fixture at the top of the nation's comedy parade as a direct result of his success with the television series. It also encouraged the men behind the Minstrels to explore new territories with the show and Don became an important part of that development. His years of experience in handling club audiences had persuaded George Mitchell and Robert Luff to try out a club adaptation of the show. The results opened a whole new dimension and packed out the Midland and Northern clubs with a six-week tour. There was a slight element of risk involved in the venture but before the opening night had finished in Wakefield, Yorkshire four further managers of large clubs were fighting to get bookings.

Don remained very philosophical about his phenomenal success with the Black and White Minstrels, considering himself fortunate to be part of a show with such an international reputation. During the hugely successful Blackpool season he told *The Stage*:

> *I don't kid myself that I fill the place every night. But if only a small percentage come in just to see me, then I feel that I have achieved something. It's an added bonus if they come to see the show and go away having enjoyed my act. I have yet to have a bad season in Blackpool and I regard this year as my best ever from both a professional and personal point of view.'*

The five years working on 'Crackerjack' and with the Minstrels had provided Don Maclean with considerable exposure on television, stage and in the media. Many were convinced that he had made the final ascent to the top of the showbusiness ladder. There were moments when Don himself was tempted to share that confidence but its effects were short-lived. Deep down inside, his fierce ambition would not abate. In order to convince himself that he had finally made it to the top, he wanted something more than he had already achieved. He knew that he had hold of the top rung of the ladder but he wanted to feel secure on his feet and remove any danger of falling. Toni and the family shared in his frustrations, supporting him at every stage. They were a strong working team, determined not to be broken under the pressures. They had seen relationship casualties spread along the wayside of the showbusiness road and had no intentions of adding to those numbers. As a family they shared their joys and frustrations but, most importantly of all, they stuck to their policy decision to be together. Don was determined—perhaps even obsessed, at times—to seal his success in some way or another. But whatever that obsession would cost him, his family were clearly not going to be part of the sacrifice.

9

Family Will Travel

Since meeting Don, Toni Maclean can hardly remember a period of time in her life when she hasn't travelled considerable numbers of miles accompanying him on a work commitment of one kind or another. It has become as natural a part of their lifestyle as a nine to five routine is for millions of other married couples. Soon after their decision to marry, they made a further commitment in deciding that they would become a team in the world of show business, actively supporting each other, sharing in the ups and downs by being together at every conceivable opportunity. It became one of the most important factors in strengthening their relationship, in a business known to break rather than make marriages.

When Don and Toni Maclean took their marriage vows they knew that they were making promises for life. Almost thirty years later their relationship remains unwavering in its commitment firstly to each other, secondly to their children and thirdly, to the business that they share. There have never been any doubts concerning the priorities in their life and the lifestyle that has emerged over those years clearly reflects these precedences. What may appear to most as crazy, disjointed and flamboyant is simply a normal routine for them. They have never known anything different and have built into it deep and strong foundations. Don made the conscious decision to invest in values and people with lasting qualities. The values were firmly rooted in his faith and the people those who, at the end of every day, would receive him unconditionally. He has clearly reaped the fruit of his investment many times over.

Rachel and Rory arrived in the second and fifth year of Don and Toni's marriage, coinciding with one of the busiest times in his career. Summer seasons and pantomimes were plentiful and television opportunities increasing. If ever the demands and pressures of the job had been strong enough to warrant Don travelling alone, like so many of his con-temporaries in the business, without the added concern of caring for wife and children, that could well have been the time. But the thought never crossed his mind. Don clearly remembers the day Bob Monkhouse offered him advice. They were having lunch together at Bob's home, enjoying watching the children playing in the swimming pool, when Bob said, 'Don, never let other people have the pleasure of seeing your children grow up.' They were words that penetrated deep into his heart, confirming his decision that the family should remain together as often as they could. The decision brought with it thousands of miles of travel, dozens of temporary homes, frequent changes of school for the children, considerable extra costs in travel and accommodation and a lot of media attention, often placing Toni and the children in a limelight that they might well have been spared had they remained at their Birmingham base. But the benefits far outweighed the costs in every respect. Don had no intention of becoming a part-time parent and stuck vehemently to his conviction that emotional stability and security in children comes as a result of families being together.

Toni simply accepted the regular upheaval as a way of life, learning to cope with the routine just as if it were a weekly trip to the supermarket. When the children were born the car got bigger and its contents increased. She always preferred to take her own personal items from the kitchen, never knowing quite what she would find in their rented accommodation. The list lengthened as the years went on and eventually included everything from a sharp vegetable knife to a washing machine and a small freezer. An assortment of clothes ranging from wellington boots to bikinis were also packed, in preparation for the very unpredictable British weather. They always made a point of purchasing large estate cars in order to cope with the volume of luggage. It was Toni's policy to create home wherever they lived and over the years she developed a fine art of doing so. Familiar rugs or lamps, their own bedding and personal kitchen items (large and small) all helped. Home for this family, was definitely where the heart was. And as long as they were together, they were all 'at home'.

Most of the time the children coped well, encouraged by their parents to accept constant moving as a normal part of their lives. During their pre-school years they were too young to realize or understand what was happening, simply being content as long as they were with Mum and Dad. When in Birmingham, they became part of the resident community on their small estate in Selly Oak, relating to neighbours and friends in the same way as other local children. As babies and toddlers they grew familiar with many of Don's dressing rooms and the stage wings, regularly standing with Toni to watch Dad perform his act. Other members of the company became part of their extended family for that particular show or season and it was always a bonus when other performers had their own children with them too. It was the longer running summer and pantomime seasons that had the lasting impact upon both Rachel and Rory. They were always welcomed backstage and when she was as young as three, Rachel would visit the theatre with her dad on an almost daily basis. One particular summer stands out in Don's memory. He was appearing at Blackpool's Opera House with Cilla Black. Rory had been born just days before the show started and so Toni was very tied to feeding and generally caring for Rachel's baby brother. They had rented a flat quite central to Blackpool and close by the theatre enabling Don to help out by taking Rachel into the theatre several times

times a week. A routine slowly built up which became a very special time for them both.

Don's was the first act on stage, after which his presence wasn't required until the finale. Rachel accompanied her Dad to the theatre in time for him to prepare for the first house at 6.15p.m. It was a particularly friendly company which always enjoyed her being there. Bill Hetterley, the stage director, had a very high stool placed just inside the wings, on which Rachel would sit whilst Don went out to do his spot. As soon as he had finished they would venture out of the theatre into the wider Winter Gardens complex where there was a fairground, stopping only to call into the dressing room to collect a pair of dark glasses in order to cover up Don's stage make-up. Together they would spend a happy hour on the many roundabouts and rides, until it was time for Don to return for the finale. Once more Rachel would sit upon her stool, carefully guarded by Bill Hetterley (who eventually went on to become head of casting with Southern TV). The gap between houses was just fifteen to twenty minutes, long enough to empty and refill the auditorium and allowing Don time to give Rachel a drink and a biscuit before beginning the whole process again. Rachel never fidgeted throughout a performance, quietly content and happy to watch her father perform. Following his second house solo spot, Don would return to their rented flat, put Rachel to bed and enjoy a coffee and a chat with Toni before returning for his second finale of the evening. It was a routine that suited the whole family well and made that particular season a special time for father and daughter.

Many of the summer and pantomime seasons during Rachel and Rory's early years had their magic moments. As young children it often felt to them as if they were part of one large extended family. The very presence of the Maclean family often helped speed up that process. Many of the dancers and up-and-coming artists were just teenagers themselves, often experiencing life away from home for the first time. They valued the presence of surrogate parents and small children who frequently served as ice-breakers in the early days of getting to know one another. Rachel and Rory spent many a season hero-worshipping the young dancers and vocalists and thrived on the attention they received from them. Jeff Thacker, now a top choreographer with the BBC, served as head chorus boy in the Young Generation dancing troupe for one summer season in Torquay. Rachel devoted her entire time to caring for his every need. At the tender age of nine years she was completely smitten by her hero, waiting night after night for him to come off the stage so that she might wipe his perspiring brow. With over twenty-six dancers in the Black and White Minstrels troupe there was never a shortage of entertainers. Ted Darling, Les Rawlings and Les Want remain particularly special in her memory of those years.

Looking back now Rachel is full of amazement and gratitude for the time, energy and patience so freely given by many of these performers to both her and Rory as young children. Many had travelled long distances from home and were unable to return during the prolonged season, thus increasing the sense of community created among fellow artists. (In latter years much of that spirit has been lost in the cost-cutting exercises of employing as many locals as possible in order to reduce expenditure on accommodation.) Don was frequently the instigator of football or cricket matches, picnics and days on the beach as well as a regular night out together, ensuring that no one was left out. Certain venues such as Torquay and Paington each had their own special events, which became welcome rituals as the years went by and Don found himself returning to ground that was becoming familiar not only to him but also to the children. Rachel and Rory were always eager to be part of these social occasions, even to the degree of wanting to attend the evening functions that Don and Toni considered far too late, long and inappropriate for children. Rachel vividly recalls giving babysitters a hard time simply because she was not allowed to be part of the night-time scene! She'd frequently plague them until Don and Toni returned in the early hours of the morning.

School years brought a slightly different perspective on life for the Maclean children. It was the first time they had really been individually affected by having a 'famous' father. The situation was made all the more intense because when both children began school Don was appearing regularly on 'Crackerjack'. Up until that point everyone they had come into contact with had been people in the business or close friends and family. All of a sudden they were the centre of intrigue and fascination. 'What's it like having a famous dad?' children would ask or 'Are you millionaires?' Rachel can recall being quite perplexed by the questions, feeling quite sure that her Dad was perfectly normal and knowing full well that he was not a millionaire. Don had instilled into them both the importance of handling money carefully, teaching them how to budget and save from a very young age. They had never been showered with lavish or luxurious gifts and the simple lifestyle adopted by Toni and Don early on in their marriage had been continued when Rachel and Rory were born. Both children recall being encouraged to save pocket money in order to buy a much longed-for toy and during one particular summer season Don actually took them into the shop and asked the owner if they could pay a little off each week until the items were paid for. He gladly agreed, enjoying watching the children reach their goal with a tremendous sense of achievement when they finally took away their models of Wonder Woman and the Incredible Hulk. Having been bred on such experiences the automatic assumption of other children that they were very wealthy both puzzled and irritated them, especially when they witnessed many schoolfriends handle money in a far more casual manner.

Local schoolchildren at St Augustine's Primary School in Solihull got used to having Rachel and Rory around and Don at the school gate and they were treated just like any other family.

Even when he had been working late and had travelled home in the early hours of the morning Don would snatch a few hours' sleep and get up early to take both children to school. Working during the latter part of the evenings meant that he was often able to collect them in the afternoon too, spending two or three hours with them before having to go off to work. Don recognized some of the advantages of this unusual lifestyle which enabled him to have quality time with the children during the early years of their life. Rachel and Rory were also well aware of the benefits, being among the few children in their school who had a father both at the school gate and also at home during the day. They frequently became the envy of their school-friends, particularly on special occasions like school concerts and their birthdays when Don would thrive on creating fun-packed parties. The theme parties were often the talk of the school for days after, not because they were particularly grand or original but purely because all the children had had such a good time being entertained by Don Maclean.

Don has always been passionate about parenting, frequently telling the children that he would give them the two things that money can't buy—his time and his love—and he knew that these could not be offered from a distance. Whenever possible he would travel home every night to be with the family. It was one of the very good reasons for staying in Birmingham, with its central location and excellent air, rail and road network enabling him to travel from virtually any point in the country in just a few hours. On rare occasions, when absolutely necessary, he might agree to stay in a hotel for a night or two but always hated having to do so. If an engagement meant him being away for more than a few nights, he'd often turn it down rather than be separated from Toni and the children. Consequently when the seasonal work came around twice a year, the family always went too. Whilst many showbusiness families would take rented accommodation during the six-week school holidays and perhaps over the main

Christmas period in pantomime, few with school-age children would come for the whole season. In the early days the summer seasons often stretched from May through to September, incorporating from six to eight weeks of school term time. For that period Don and Toni would always register Rachel and Rory in a local school close to the theatre and their rented accommodation.

Rachel thrived on the challenge of making new friends, having inherited her father's outgoing personality. Being the new girl and often the centre of attention was great fun and provided her with the perfect stage on which to display her gifts and talents. She was showing early signs of following in her father's footsteps as a scholar, sportswoman and performer, frequently stealing the limelight both in and out of school. She hardly needed the prestige of being the daughter of a celebrity, being quite confident in building up her own relationships. She once told the press, at the tender age of nine, 'I don't talk about my father. I'm very proud of him but I want to be liked for being me.' During Don's 'Crackerjack' heyday she did struggle a little with the constant bombardment of children shouting 'Crackerjack' every time they went out of the house. He was regularly besieged by autograph hunters, which often delayed family shopping trips or play times in the park when the Macleans were simply going about their everyday life trying to be a normal family. There were even occasions when children would cycle to their house in Selly Oak and demand that Don came to the door to see them, which made family teatimes difficult to cope with. Rachel had been known to stand in front of Don at such times, stretching her arms out wide in protection of him whilst declaring to the world at large, ' He's *my* daddy!'

It was particularly hard when they were trying to snatch some quality hours during the hectic summer seasons. Rory and Rachel loved their family times together on the beach and nothing infuriated Rachel more than having to share her Dad with dozens of other children. Don remembers one particular day in Blackpool when several children had thrust pens and paper in front of his nose demanding autographs. Being aware of the children's feelings at such times, he cast an eye in their direction to see how they were reacting, only to discover Rachel confidently signing her own autographs! She had finally adopted the attitude, 'If you can't beat him, join him!' It wasn't many years before Rachel literally did join her father on stage.

The constant move of schools became quite an ordeal for Rory, who was much quieter and more reserved than his sister, often preferring his own company to that of crowds of other children. School was never his most favourite place even in the secure environment of Solihull, so what became an annual change of teacher and classmates brought its fair share of trauma to the youngster's life. Having a famous Dad intensified the problem. Girls would run up to Rory and give him a kiss saying, 'Give that to your Dad,' and their constant barrage of questions made him want to retreat. Being the focus of attention affected him quite differently from Rachel although he was always grateful that she was only a classroom or two away. At one stage Rory resisted going to school at all and refused all invitations to play out or visit friends' homes. Don and Toni became quite concerned and tried everything within their powers to help him to make friends and overcome his acute shyness. He can actually remember thinking that he must have been adopted into the family because he was so obviously different from the three extroverts who shared in his life.

One particular year Don and Toni took the very radical decision to teach him at home during the summer season, rather than send him to another new school. His Birmingham teachers were most supportive of the decision and helped in every way they could by suggesting topics, projects and books that the family could use in their learning times together. To this day Rory can recall the books he read and the topics covered during that summer season. It turned out to be one of the happiest times away, with both children thoroughly enjoying

Dad as teacher and more importantly Rory gaining a lot of self- confidence. It was also around this time that he discovered a passion for rugby. As part of Don's plan to help his son overcome his shyness and make friends, he took him down to their local rugby club's junior section. Whilst he was initially reluctant to go, the experience became a turning point in Rory's life and has remained the single most influential factor determining his social life, hobby and choice of career. And his greatest fan, supporter and friend through it all has remained his father.

Despite the intrusion into family privacy there was definitely a positive side to being part of a celebrity family that Rachel and Rory both enjoyed. The long list of charity events that so often accompanied summer seasons made being part of a famous family distinctly advantageous. Local fairs, fêtes and garden parties loved the family image that the Macleans freely and sincerely volunteered when agreeing to take part in the official opening ceremony. Not only did the children get to try out every ride, game or competition but they were usually taken to the front of the queue. There was always demand for autographs at such events and Don used the opportunity to raise a little more money for the charity concerned by charging ten pence for his much longed-for signature. It was Rory's job to collect and count the money—a responsibility he remembers taking very seriously—which made him feel a vital part of the event. The children thrived on being part of the family business in this way and the public obviously delighted in them too.

Christmases at home in Selly Oak and later Solihull were rare, especially during the period when Don was working on 'Crackerjack'. The 1976 pantomime at Wolverhampton's Grand Theatre became Rory's very first Christmas in his own home. He was almost five years of age. Just occasionally Don scooped a Midlands pantomime, which enabled the family to enjoy their familiar surroundings and invite extended family and friends round to celebrate. A family visit to the Christmas Eve performance of whatever pantomime Don was appearing in had become a well-established tradition, followed by a party packed with food and fun. Nothing delighted Don and Toni more than being able to share their home with family and close friends. Being part of a community of people has always been very important to the Macleans, whether it's family, neighbours or a company of artists and performers. The festive occasions were important times of sharing and being with others.

Don's parents only lived a short distance away and there was never a week, when at home, that he didn't call in and visit them. It had always been his ambition to buy them their own home and move them out of the rapidly changing district of Sparkbrook. The peak years of 'Crackerjack' and the Minstrels finally provided Don with the financial means to do that and nothing could have delighted him more. Moving away from the place which had been home to them for nearly thirty-five years, leaving friends and neighbours behind, was a major event in Rosie and Charles Maclean's life and Don marked the occasion by throwing a party for them to say goodbye. It was a wonderful night with everyone enjoying some good food and drink, not least Charles Maclean. Feeling very relaxed and enjoying an unusual freedom in his conversation, he chose that evening to tell Don that he had always had very different ambitions for his son. 'You've been a great disappointment to me, son. You should have stayed on at school and become a sports master in a Grammar School,' he spluttered as Don was helping him into the car ready to return home. The news took Don by complete surprise as he had never suspected that his father had held such secret ambitions for him. For a short while it cast a slight shadow on the evening but in time and on reflection that lifted as Don knew full well that his father had thoroughly enjoyed his son's success as an entertainer and had relished many moments of parental pride over the years.

Pride as a parent is one sin that Don has very little con-science about. Personality profiles, documentary programmes and articles over the years have quoted him saying on many an occasion, 'I am the world's best father.' He also confesses to being a 'heavy-handed' father, not in the sense that he ever had the need or desire to exert physical punishment on his children but more in the conviction that children find their security in firm parenting and knowing exactly where their boundary lines lie. As adults both Rory and Rachel willingly testify to the firm way in which they were raised as small children and teenagers. Their moral and ethical foundations were, like Don's own, firmly rooted in the Catholic Church. Attending mass was a family occasion enjoyed by them all, which continues to be an important part of the two children's lives as adults. They have always known the support and encouragement of their parents at every stage of their lives. Whatever activity or interest they were involved in, Don and Toni always shared in it.

Rachel spent hours and hours competing in gymnastics competitions and swimming galas, with Don fitting his work schedule around both the training sessions and competition times. Later, during her early teens, she set her own heart on following her father into the business, concentrating on developing her gifts as a singer, dancer and actress. When the occasion arose, father and daughter would share the stage singing duets together. They became well known for their rendering of the popular Frank and Nancy Sinatra number, 'Something Stupid'. Modelling agencies also signed her up onto their books, offering her a wide range of promotion and fashion work, all of which was very carefully monitored by her parents. Despite knowing the pitfalls and dangers of the world of show business, Don never discouraged Rachel during this time. As she approached sixteen years of age, he told her that if she found work on the stage he would allow her to leave school rather than staying on into the sixth form to study for 'A' levels. Rachel landed herself with a part in a touring stage production of *Hansel and Gretel*, followed by several small parts in other plays and musicals. At the tender age of sixteen she went way up on the north-east coast and did her first pantomime in Sunderland, working alongside Paul Shane. It was a daunting experience and also meant a Christmas away from the family but just as her family had so often offered friendship and companionship to youngsters in the business, she found herself on the receiving end of surrogate parenting and the spirit of friendship amongst the company.

Just occasionally Rachel found employment working alongside Don as assistant stage manager with a theatre company. Her insights into the world of show business had given her a true perspective of the type of determination and perseverance that would be required in order to succeed. After a couple of years working in the business, she knew that drive within her wasn't strong enough and decided to pursue alternative career options, which allowed her the freedom to use her performing gifts in the world of amateur dramatics.

Nothing pleased Don more than being able to involve his family in his work. In the late eighties during their teenage years a television opportunity came his way that enabled them all to be actively involved in the making of a very successful ATV series called 'Supersavers' (ATV was the forerunner of Central TV). Don maintains that he was the ideal choice for a show aimed at encouraging people to learn new skills in order to economise. He confesses to being absolutely useless around the house, especially when it comes to DIY. The lunch-time series, which ran for ten weeks, had all four of them looking closely at what they bought in the supermarket and bargain-hunting for clothes and second-hand furniture, as well as learning about household electrics and the basic mechanics of a car. It proved to be a successful series and an enjoyable experience for Don, Toni and the children, with the media once more delighting in the sincere and genuine image of this showbusiness family.

Robert Holmes was the man officially responsible for promoting Don in the media. After leaving journalism and joining the public relations company George Bartram Associates Don had become his first client. It was when his career was very much in the ascendancy and he was enjoying the high profile of 'Crackerjack' and the Minstrels. Robert struck up an excellent working relationship with Don which over twenty-five years has developed into a close family friendship. He says that representing Don has always been a tremendous pleasure with there never being the slightest hint of scandal to deal with or the need to fabricate a story or cover-up for him. Don's public image has never been anything other than that of a good, moral, family man whose hard labour has brought continual work and success and Robert knows that the public and private man is consistently the same.

As the children got older and their education became more critical, the family travelled less and less. Don's work routine changed in order to be at home for as much of the time as he could. On the few occasions when he did have to stay away, there would never be a day when he didn't speak with them all by phone. He proudly informs journalists that 'my family remain the most important people in my life. I can go out and get no laughs at all but when I come home it will be exactly as I left it. They're not going to care whether I've failed or not. That's my solid base and they're not going to leave me no matter what.' And there's no question of Don ever leaving them either.

10

Forty and Famous?

The decision in 1977 to come out of 'Crackerjack' was not an easy one for Don. The popular children's show, along with the Black and White Minstrels, had dominated five years of his professional and personal world, making him a household name and bringing considerable financial security into his life. Only Leslie Crowther and Peter Glaze had worked as part of the team for longer. But Don was beginning to feel trapped and uncomfortable. Despite all his work with the Minstrels he had convinced himself that the public and producers were beginning to label him as a children's presenter. He had enjoyed 'Crackerjack' but had no desire to become the country's second John Noakes—of Blue Peter fame—and felt the need to return to the world of adult audiences. He talked with friends and colleagues but there appeared to be no clear consensus of opinion as to whether he should take the big step in declining a fifth contract with the show. Billy Cotton Jnr, the then Head of Light Entertainment at the BBC, was very keen to keep him and put considerable pressure on both Don and his agent to persuade him to stay. Others, including fellow entertainers in the world of television, had also warned him of the possible consequences of turning a major BBC contract down.

But Don continued to feel frustrated and impatient. Things weren't happening fast enough for him. He had always had his sights set on becoming an international star by the time he was thirty and had failed. The reality as he saw it was that he was rapidly approaching thirty-five, still looking for the big break to secure him in the world of television and stuck in what seemed to be a permanent fixture on a children's TV show. The frustration was intensified by some of his contemporaries who, having travelled similar paths, had found their breaks and were clearly establishing themselves among the country's leading entertainers. Cannon and Ball, Russ Abbott and others were not only appearing as guests on top shows and being interviewed by popular chat show hosts but were also now offered their own television series. Don remembers being genuinely pleased for them, knowing that they had worked hard and deserved their success but he couldn't help thinking and feeling, 'Why not me too?' He was desperate to host 'The Don Maclean Show', receive invitations from prestigious shows like 'Parkinson' and 'Saturday Night at The Mill' but as long as he was being seen first and foremost as a children's presenter he felt those opportunities would never come his way. The Minstrels had kept him in the adult eye but the attraction to that show was the whole 'Black and White' concept, not him as an individual. Don wanted a change in direction and, as it wasn't naturally coming his way, he took the courageous decision to bring it about for himself.

Morris Aza had been far more than an agent to Don. He was a true professional, a charming gentleman as well as a friend and had never offered him anything other than good advice, working tirelessly to find him the right work experience. Don's success and popularity on 'Crackerjack' was clearly going to be a hard act to follow and the pressure from the BBC for him to continue put his agent in a very difficult position. Morris' role was to represent the interests of his artists, not to tell them what to do and in this case he was well aware of Don's feelings.

Ultimately the decision was Don's. Morris tried hard to negotiate with the BBC and at one stage went with Don to talk about the possibility of him hosting a show of his own. The discussions were difficult and they showed little enthusiasm, turning to Don at one stage asking, 'What can you offer us that Dick Emery can't?' This rhetorical question finally made Don realize that he was not going to get his own programme. He came home feeling a mixture of anger, disappointment and determination still to make his mark at the top of the entertainment world somehow. After much deliberation he asked Morris to negotiate for a renewed contract for the Black and Whites but not 'Crackerjack'. The BBC's response was short but not sweet: they made it quite clear that the choice was either both or neither. Don recalls Morris encouraging him to reconsider the options carefully before making a final decision but his mind was made up. One way or another, he was determined to get the television break that he wanted, even if it meant doing so without the assistance of the BBC. It wasn't until much later and in hindsight, that he fully realized the implications of his decision. It was little comfort to discover that he had not been alone in his fight against the system—other stars of that period also found themselves unable to beat it.

Fellow comedians were sympathetic with Don's plight and none more so than Bob Monkhouse. In the months following Don's withdrawal from 'Crackerjack' Bob helped him to stay in the television frame through occasional appearances on ITV's 'Celebrity Squares'. Having suddenly been wiped from the BBC screen Don was concerned to keep his face in the public eye and 'Celebrity Squares' helped not only in its exposure but also in placing him alongside other well-established personalities. The two men worked well together and had a mutual respect for each other's performances as comedians. Don admired the diversity of skills in Bob as both a writer and performer, often describing him as 'the Noel Coward of our age'. It was through a programme called 'Comedy Connections', written by Bob Monkhouse and Colin Bostock-Smith, that Don saw his first big opportunity since leaving 'Crackerjack'. ATV commissioned the comedy series based upon an outline that Bob had submitted. Don, in Bob's own words, was 'the lynchpin of my invention'.

The idea of the show was to spin a small group of clever comedians, including Derek Hobson, Dave Ismay and Pat Mills, through a range of different sketches. At the centre of these scenes was Comic Control, a pivotal point from which a frenzied Don ruled over the comings and goings of this crazy gang. Four doors led to four different rooms off the central point that Don controlled. Once through a door each comedian entered a variety of different settings and immediately switched into the sketches. Bob recalls:

> *It was a daring project of disparate styles and gags, all requiring discipline to hold it together and, above all, an axial figure at its focal point of great vitality and charm. To my mind Don was the only man in Britain for that role. The resulting pilot show was a personal triumph for Don. He was at once the domineering ringmaster, mad professor and wisecracking wizard of oscillation. What could have happened with such a vehicle for Don's most manic magic one can only surmise.*

The world was left surmising, as the pilot programme was dismissed as being far 'too nutsy' by one influential bigwig from New York, after which the first series of nine programmes was cancelled. Having been contracted for the whole series, every-one was paid off and told not to come in again. The audience ratings for the pilot had been extraordinarily high, leaving everyone somewhat puzzled and confused by the decision. The exercise had not been a cheap one for ATV but far more costly was the disappointment experienced by all who had taken part, not least Don, who had started to think that he had found the ideal platform on which to prove his worth. It was only much later that Bob Monkhouse learned that the very same New York bigwig had also dismissed 'Monty Python's Flying Circus'.

Fortunately BBC radio was quite separate from BBC television and Don was never out of work during this period, appearing in several very popular and highly-rated comedy programmes. His first passion was undoubtedly television but radio clearly loved him and offers of work were never far away. He had been enjoying a regular appearance on the Radio 2 programme 'Wit's End', working with producer Danny Greenstone, who later went on to work for Grundy Television. This radio variety showcase promoted several stars in its day and Don had enjoyed his frequent appearances, once more employing the skills of friend and writer Howard Imber. When television failed to offer him the opportunity for his own show, radio succeeded on more than one occasion. Writer Tony Hare created the first of these in Pebble Mill Radio's first ever situation comedy, with the celebrated title 'Maclean Up Britain'. Originally the BBC intended to make the show in a London studio but Don argued strongly for it to be recorded from his home town of Birmingham, providing Pebble Mill with their debut in situation comedy. It became an enormous success.

'Maclean Up Britain' had a ring of the great days of radio comedy that Don had been bred on with echoes of 'Round the Horne' and yet it offered a unique style and pace that was anything but old-fashioned with scripts that were both fresh and funny. Best described as a science fiction comedy, it focused on the antics of a mad professor called Pontius Maclean, played by Don, who found himself characteristically engaged in a wide variety of adventures including driving a hovercraft, swinging from the bells of Notre Dame and diving in a submarine. The audiences at Pebble Mill were enormously supportive, not least because the star was one of their very own. The supporting cast included Chris Emmett, Bob Todd and Jan Hunt, who had also found fame through her work with 'Crackerjack'. The bizarre, half-hour, Goon-like situation comedies gathered a regular following with excellent listening figures. One of the journalists from the *Daily Mirror* selected it as his 'pick of the week' for every week of its entire run, providing a regular coverage of the antics of the mad Professor

Pontius. The BBC were delighted with the show's success and made immediate plans to invest further in Don's popularity and skills but instead of another series the producer suggested a revue-type show based on a succession of short comedy sketches. What emerged was a sketch show called 'Keep it Maclean', quite different from the Goon-style situation comedy of 'Maclean Up Britain'. Whilst it included many of the same cast from 'Maclean Up Britain', Tony Hare was joined by fellow writers Howard Imber, Jimmy Mulville and Rory McGrath. Together they produced several series which went from strength to strength, enjoying popular Sunday lunchtime listening with repeats going out on Fridays. All in all there was rarely a week when Don wasn't performing comedy on the radio. Whilst at one time the route for great successful comics like the Goons and Tony Hancock was from radio into television, Don seemed to be reversing the order, going from TV recognition to enormous success on radio. His bouncy personality, immediately identifiable voice and razor-sharp wit communicated effectively through this medium, successfully entertaining thousands of listeners.

Despite success on radio Don's television bug would not abate. He continued to push hard at doors both at the BBC and ITV. Having built up numbers of contacts over the years at the Pebble Mill television studios, he had hoped that some regional work might come his way. Eventually he took an idea for a comedy programme to them. It was a simple concept, using the minimum of staging, props and costumes and appropriately called 'The Cheapest Show on the Telly'. Don was convinced that he was onto a winner, having devised something that was quite different to anything he had ever done on television before. Right from the start he had one other comedian in mind to appear with him—the then up-and-coming Lenny Henry. Lenny first came into the national limelight through 'New Faces' in 1975 as the first schoolboy winner of this popular talent competition. Following this success Bob Luff of the Black and

White Minstrels signed him up for the Blackpool summer show, carefully placing him under Don's experienced eye. Lenny was an original, fresh but very young and raw performer. Blackpool, potentially, was a big break for him. He had little experience of live audiences and none of the background of clubs and holiday camps that had been Don's training ground. For the first few weeks of the show Don did all that he could to support and encourage the young performer, even to the extent of going to the back of the auditorium to watch Lenny's performance and taking notes as to when and where he was and wasn't, getting laughs. During the interval they would go through the act, looking at ways in which it could be improved and developed in preparation for the second house. Don helped Lenny to shape his act and develop style and greater depth as a performer in those early days. Lenny was a fast learner and enjoyed great success as a result of the Blackpool season. He and Don went on to enjoy working together in the Minstrels' tour of the clubs the following autumn. When, a few years later Don was looking for a partner in 'Cheapest Show' he felt sure that, along with Howard Imber's writing skills, they had a team guaranteed to succeed. And he wasn't wrong.

The two comedians combined well to make what the press recognized as one of the most successful regional TV programmes to come out of Pebble Mill for some time. Producer John Clarke saw them as the ideal combination for a professional team and at the same time, nicely contrasted in style. It was an unusual kind of comedy, blending Don's experience and lightning wit with Lenny's gifted spontaneity and freshness. On stage they produced a chemistry that was very successful and off-stage their friendship sparked numerous ideas with Lenny openly admitting to the press that he was learning a lot from Don's many years of experience in the business and benefitting from the advice that he offered. Some began to talk of them as a double act but both were quick to defend their own individual styles and intentions to remain as solo performers. The simplicity of the show highlighted their individual talents. There were very few costumes or props to aid their performance. Initially for the pilot programme, they worked out of a small newsreaders' studio with an audience of only thirty people. They wore simple black and white trousers and shirts, regularly introducing themselves as 'the white one wearing black and white and the black one wearing white and black'. The only change of costume throughout the show was hats, used in order to indicate a change of character. Many of the sketches were written and first rehearsed in the Macleans' Solihull home where Lenny had become a frequent welcome visitor to the family and an adopted 'Uncle Lenny' to Rachel and Rory. It became a hugely successful working partnership which reaped its fruit not only in delighting Pebble Mill's regional audiences but in attracting the interest of London producers with a view to networking the show nationally.

Robin Nash, ex-producer of 'Crackerjack', was now head of Light Entertainment at the BBC. He invited Don down to London to discuss various possibilities in relation to 'Cheapest Show'. Once again, Don was hoping that this might turn out to be the programme to give him the national TV status and exposure he had failed to find when leaving 'Crackerjack' but it wasn't to be. Producer Ernest Maxim had been looking for the right kind of platform on which to present several up-and-coming young artists and recognized that 'Cheapest Show' might very well be ideal to do that. He proposed that the cast increased from two to six and moved to a much bigger London studio, in order to increase the audience size.

Don was not convinced that the changes would work and returned to Birmingham in order to talk things over with Lenny and Howard. 'Cheapest Show' was the closest he had ever come to talking with the BBC about a show that would almost be his and Lenny's very own. The thought of becoming just two of six personalities that would appear in a show under a different title didn't appeal to him. Don felt sure that if they held out for a while the BBC would eventually take the original package. Lenny wasn't so confident. He was young, enthusiastic and eager to take any TV offer he could get and eventually persuaded Don to agree to the BBC's suggestion of what became known as 'Six of a Kind'. The four additional artists included comedian David Copperfield, singer Leah Bell, dancer Pearly Gates and impressionist Karen Kaye. The BBC commissioned a series of six shows and the new team, with Howard Imber remaining as one of their writers, enjoyed several weeks working together.

Around that time one of the BBC unions called a strike over pay and conditions of work. All programmes were disrupted and many new ones were delayed in being screened. Don waited patiently to hear when 'Six of a Kind' was to be shown but no news came and time dragged on. He kept ringing to find out what was happening but was fobbed off with a different excuse each time. 'Six of a Kind' never did see the light of day. It was like reliving the disappointment of 'Comedy Connections' six times over. No explanation was ever offered and to this day Don has never fully understood why the BBC should plough so much money into making so many programmes and not screen them. Seemingly they had money to throw away.

It was over two years later when the BBC announced the arrival of a new comedy show called 'Three of a Kind'. It included Lenny Henry, David Copperfield and a then new artist by the name of Tracey Ullman. Don could hardly believe what he was hearing. There was no doubt in his mind that this was 'The Cheapest Show on Telly', twice renamed. He had been excluded along with three of the cast of 'Six of a Kind'. To make matters even more painful, it became a phenomenal success. They went on to make several series, all of which helped launch Tracey Ullman as one of the most successful comedy artists of the day and played a big part in guaranteeing Lenny a secure future in television. However, Don has never been one to begrudge another's success. In many ways nobody could have been more delighted than he was to see Lenny's climb to the top of the showbusiness ladder, knowing that he had given a helping hand on the way. Yes, he was sorry not to have been the one to experience the growth in what had been essentially his baby but more than fifteen years late, he adopts a very philosophical view of the matter. 'At the end of the day' says Don 'that's show business.' What saddens him most is not that his ideas were taken and used to bring success for others but simply the fact that he wasn't told that it was going to happen. He would like to have known.

Don wasn't the only one to feel the disappointment of 'Cheapest Show'. Howard Imber had turned full-time writer during its successful run at Pebble Mill. He clearly recognized that his own success as a writer had been greatly helped by the regular work Don had given him as well as the many contacts with TV companies and individuals he had gained through knowing Don. His decision to go full-time was strongly influenced by Don employing him to write on a regular basis and offering him a monthly retainer. They were also good friends with a deep respect for each other's work. When Don was dropped and 'Three of a Kind' came to the surface, Howard, having been retained as a writer on the show, found the situation somewhat embarrassing. Whilst still loyal to Don, he had by now, through 'Cheapest Show', developed not only a friendship with Lenny but also a professional partnership. Naturally Howard was very happy for Lenny but at the same time desperately disappointed for Don. Thanks to Don his own career was still moving forward apace but it was hard to see the one who had helped set it in motion miss out in this way. Howard could sense Don's frustration and disappointment and longed to see him get the breaks that so many people in the business felt he deserved. He always worried that Don tried too hard to succeed, especially where television was concerned. It had become a compulsive obsession in his life which was in danger of working against, rather than for, his cause.

Morris Aza also recalls Don's desperation and constant preoccupation with the need to be on television. As his agent he felt quite exasperated by Don's continual hounding for the big break opportunity and then his further disappointment when it wasn't forthcoming. One other hugely successful comedian who worked for many years in theatre and clubs without success in television was Ken Dodd. Morris saw many similarities in their exhaustive styles of working. Don's act was also high-speed, full of movement and expression, with loud extravagant gestures not easily adapted to the small screen. He clearly struggled to translate the kind of comedy that he was so successful with on stage to the television and many of his determined efforts in a stand-up comic role had failed to do him justice. Don was never short of work but Morris just couldn't provide the opportunities to satisfy his insatiable appetite for television. It led to a difficult period in their long-standing working relationship.

Don became convinced that the agents who succeeded in getting their artists onto television were those who already had clients working regularly for the TV companies. As he saw it, at that time, Morris wasn't able to create those openings and so he decided to move on to a new agency. It had been a happy and successful working partnership for almost fifteen years and one that Morris Aza was especially sorry to see end. He had thoroughly enjoyed representing Don, liked him as a person and believed sincerely in him as a performer. He hoped that he would find what he was looking for.

As was the case in leaving 'Crackerjack', the decision to part company with Aza Artists is, with the experience of hindsight, one that Don regrets. He doesn't think that his career would have been particularly enhanced by staying with the agency but now realizes that neither would it have been restricted. Don enjoyed a quality and depth of relationship with Morris Aza that he has not found elsewhere. He recognizes that he was young and hot-headed and wishes that Morris had been much firmer and more directive with him but that was not a role that the experienced agent chose to play with his client. Years later, Don retains a degree of sadness about his decision at that time.

The move to Paul Vaughan Associates produced a lot of work but no great miracle results in television. ATV's 'Super Savers', the popular series which taught people to spend economically and wisely, had been enormously successful as a programme but had its limitations. Don thoroughly enjoyed making it and loved the involvement of Toni and the family but it achieved very little in terms of promoting him as a comedy entertainer. However his light, offbeat, humorous style of presenting had gone down well and there was no doubt that producers were beginning to see him in quite a different light. Other opportunities quickly followed with several one-off BBC regional documentary-style programmes coming his way. Success in these led to three series of a programme called 'Keen Types' produced by John Clarke from Pebble Mill. Don's versatility as host, presenter, interviewer and general-purpose man was welcomed by producers and audiences alike. He was an ideal choice for a programme focusing on ordinary people with unusual hobbies. As a man full of energy with engrossing hobbies of his own, he took a genuine interest in collectors of military-style vehicles, Gilbert and Sullivan fans, people who dress up as cowboy and Indians and others with rather unusual and obsessive interests.

Despite his continued success in pantomime and summer seasons and several low-key television programmes, Don made it clear that he still craved the one big-time show. He was the first to admit that it wasn't coming his way and the advent of his fortieth birthday was slowly having an effect upon him.

Life became quite strained for a while and the added pressure of his father's illness with cancer of the bowel cast a grey shadow over Don's life. He had been able to support his father through a prolonged period of hospitalization and major surgery. He visited daily, sat with him for the hours building up to the operation and was there for him when he came round from the anaesthetic. He prayed hard and sought the prayers of others for his father during this period. The operation's success meant that Charles Maclean was able to enjoy five more good years before having to return for further surgery. Rosie Maclean did not cope at all well with her husband's illness. They both knew that he was suffering from cancer but neither could bring themselves to talk openly about it. During his prolonged periods of hospitalization she became very reliant upon Don and Toni even to the point of moving into their home to live with them. The second, less serious operation coincided with Don being on tour and he was unable to be at the hospital to support his father through this time. Don lives with the sadness of knowing that his father never made it to the theatre on that occasion, having become very anxious and been taken seriously ill on the day he was admitted to hospital. Despite Don's attempts to get home Charles Maclean died just twenty minutes before he arrived. His father's suffering and death became another factor during these years which caused him to re-evaluate his career and life in general.

Don had never needed a lot of sleep. His high-energy performances as a comedian simply reflected the high-energy person behind the performance. But he slept even less during what, in hindsight, he recognizes as a difficult period in his life. Some might have called it a mid-life crisis but a diagnosis was of no great significance to Don. All he knew was that at forty years of age he had failed to reach the goal that he had set for himself. He was fearful of becoming an old and redundant comedian and was also beginning to fear the onset of his mother's paranoia, especially when reading through interviews that he had given. Uncharacteristically for him he developed a 'couldn't care less' attitude towards life for a few months. For the first time ever he didn't rush home at the earliest opportunity or spend every conceivable moment with Toni and the children. He bottled his feelings up inside unable to express them even to family and close friends. Don didn't like what he was experiencing and began to feel unwell, spending several nights lying awake, unable to sleep at all. On the rare occasion he did drop off he woke up bathed in perspiration and exhausted from dreams that troubled rather than comforted him. It was during one of these sleepless nights that he realized he couldn't continue in this way. He faced up to the fact that if he hadn't made it to the top of the showbusiness ladder after more than twenty years of trying, he was unlikely ever to do so. That night Don took a long and hard look at himself and his career, placed his ambition for international fame and success to one side and decided to enjoy what he was good at. He knew that he was unlikely ever to be out of a job and was still in the privileged position of being able to select carefully the kind of work that he preferred.

Don's spiritual life also took a new turn during this period. God had always played a very important role in his life and the disciplines of regular confession to a priest and faithful attendance at Sunday mass were meaningful and well integrated in his life. His faith had also provided him with a moral and ethical framework for living, one that he was determined to pass on to his children. But during these years he began to think more deeply about his faith and it became increasingly important that he should offer himself more fully to God. Don was always happy to be identified as a Roman Catholic, especially through the Catholic Stage Guild but apart from that occasional association his religious and professional lives were largely separate. He regularly prayed before a performance, asking for God's blessing on his work but rarely prayed about his career, the choices he should make and the paths he should take.

The decision to let go of his ambitions somehow enabled him to place his life in God's hands in a much more personal way. He hadn't been particularly aware of keeping God out but the experiences of the last few months had made him realize that he was now drawing closer to the God whom he had always known.

Life took on a very different perspective almost immediately and Don clearly remembers feeling relieved of a decidedly heavy burden. The fierce ambition had gone and the goal posts changed their position. He had no intentions of slowing down or working any less but found a new freedom both to choose and to enjoy what he did. As a result he feels sure that he became a much nicer person, more open to and appreciative of others he came into contact with in the business. The family had always been high on Don's agenda but around this time he made a conscious decision to enjoy his children's growing years even more. Rachel and Rory were now into secondary education and required less disruption to their lives. Don happily forfeited summer seasons to enable them to remain together as a family at their Solihull base. The children's interests and hobbies became his and he set himself goals of a very different kind, telling journalists:

> *At one time I was incredibly ambitious. But now my values are centred on my family. The important thing is for me to be my son's best friend in a few years' time and to be the sort of man my daughter would look for to marry. That would be a real achievement.*

Don's ambition had been for fame not money. He may not have succeeded in getting to the top of his professional ladder by the time he had reached his fortieth birthday but he had a growing sense in which he felt the best was yet to come. In hindsight he describes this stage as 'the watershed years', a time that clearly divides two quite separate periods in his life. The primary change was not in what he did but in him as a person although, as time went on, his work did take some unexpected turns.

11

Variety, the Spice of Life

The word that most appropriately describes Don's work commitments following his watershed experience is probably 'variety', not in the traditional sense of the variety performances that had often been part of the earlier stages of his career (although these did occasionally still feature in his schedule) but more the range and diversity of engagements that he undertook. The freedom that he now experienced released him from the pressure of feeling he had to prove anything either to himself or to the world of entertainment. He felt more contentment, greater security in the achievements he had made and less need to strive for further success. But this experience didn't remove the very different ambition to explore his own potential at greater depths. Don had a growing sense of there being parts of him that had been left dormant and he made a conscious decision to delve into what he hoped might be hidden resources that would add colour and richness to his life.

He never removed himself completely from the core of show business, not least because it continued to be his most regular source of income and pleasure. His love of live theatre audiences remained an important part of his life and there was always a demand for his experience and expertise. However, in preference to working the long traditional summer season away from home, Don took on a greater number of one-off engagements as well as shorter one- or two-week stints. None was more enjoyable than topping the bill on the *QE 2* liner. He and Toni thrived on being part of the ship's community for a week at a time, delighting hundreds of holiday-makers and thoroughly enjoying themselves in the process. Touring the various top Butlins sites around Britain's seaside resorts was more tiring in terms of travel but no less enjoyable, as Don was able to do what he loves more than anything else—be with people and make them laugh hysterically throughout their holiday. It was a constant reminder of where he had begun and it was reassuring to know that after more than twenty years in the business he continued to enthral the hundreds of folk who nightly flocked to see him.

One unexpected invitation to come his way added variety and richness to his life beyond his wildest imagination. Don had played to a wide range of people in his time, in some very differing circumstances but the experience of performing in a tent, a gun-shed and a bare village hall that had once contained 114 prisoners of war was a definite first! The chance to travel with the Combined Services Entertainment group to perform before troops serving in the Falkland Islands was a privilege that both thrilled and humbled Don. This engagement turned out to be two of the most moving weeks of his life. He flew in an RAF VC10 to Ascension Island, where the *Uganda* was anchored in the bay. *Uganda* was a cruise ship that had been commandeered as a hospital ship during the Falklands conflict and was still in service with the Royal Navy at this time. Don did two shows on Ascension Island before travelling by a Wessex helicopter to perform for the crew on board the *Uganda*. This was followed by a thirteen-hour flight on a Hercules aeroplane to the Falklands, taking him to some of the world's lesser-known stages, performing two shows a night to a crowd of 350 people cramped into a small cinema, with smaller, more informal gatherings programmed into the daytime. On his travels around the Falklands Don visited many of the now famous places where battles were fought and lives lost, including Bluff Cove—where dozens of Welsh Guardsmen were killed in an air attack on two British ships—Mount Kent and Tumbledown. Don delighted in chatting with soldiers and the islands' inhabitants, especially those who could tell their own stories of bravery and courage, many of which will never go into the history books. He felt proud to have been invited and very happy to be able to make contact with many of the people serving from his Midlands home, especially those serving with the Royal Regiment of Fusiliers formally the Royal Warwickshire Fusiliers. The *Birmingham Mail* had promised that Don would deliver any letters which arrived at the office before his departure. He left with a sack full of mail, personally delivering dozens of messages from one side of the world to the other. Before leaving, Don was also honoured to be able to lay a poppy wreath in the Falklands Military Cemetery on behalf of a Midlands association.

The only disappointment of the whole Falklands trip was that shortly after having agreed to go Don was offered a lead in Willy Russell's stage play *One for the Road* and the dates clashed. He clearly couldn't do both and had no intention of withdrawing from the Falklands. The play would have allowed him to appear in what he considered one of the country's finest repertory theatres—the Birmingham Repertory—but on his return he didn't have to wait too long before another opportunity came his way.

Dave Freeman's comedy farce *A Bedful of Foreigners* had already enjoyed a successful run in London's West End, featuring Terry Scott as the main star. When Don was offered the same leading part, Stanley, with the touring company he jumped at the chance to move into the 'legit' side of the business. The play went down especially well at Birmingham's Alexandra Theatre, featuring a double Brummie bill with Don and co-star model, actress, businesswoman and author Mandy Rice-Davies, known for the Profumo scandal of the sixties. Don regularly teased the press with the statement that he was the only man ever to be paid to get into bed with Mandy Rice-Davies once a night and twice on Saturday! The hilarious bedroom romp found the two entwined in a web of disaster, following a few wrong turns during a holiday in France. Journalists delighted in their partnership on stage and their friendship off-stage, as each discovered for the first time that they were almost neighbours. The two found that they had several things in common, not least their joint love of literature and spent many happy hours discussing plays, novels and poetry. Underneath Mandy's scandalous reputation Don discovered an intelligent, gifted and generous person. His life had been enriched through meeting her.

The tour lasted several months, stretching from one end of the country to the other and Don felt challenged by the whole experience. Initially it absorbed all his energies as he learned lines and moves as well as the discipline of sticking to them night after night. As time went on he admits to feeling restricted by the degree of repetition that performing a play requires. Not only was he unable to change the script but he had to come to terms with the fact that the others on stage with him were quite unused to a member of the cast suddenly doing something quite different. The teamwork felt much stronger and he quickly realized that one person's mistake can seriously affect another's performance. Don also had to learn to ignore his audience which, after twenty years of speaking to them and demanding a response in the process, was quite hard to get used to. But the change was refreshing and Don's performances were both appreciated by audiences and noticed by producers. Not many months after completing the tour, a second invitation came his way, this time to perform alongside the experienced actress Anne Hamilton in a Malcolm Knight production of Ray Cooney's *Chase Me Comrade*. Don describes his character in this play as that of a headless chicken dashing around the stage in a frantic performance that certainly tested his physical fitness. Playing a man of thirty, he reluctantly agreed to have his silver-grey hair dyed dark brown. The producer, Tony Clayton, convinced him that it was a simple task, frequently undertaken by many professional actors. Colouring it dark brown *was* simple but the attempt to dye it back to his natural colour at the end of the run was not so successful. Having spent literally hours in the hairdresser's salon, he eventually had to come to terms with living with purple hair for a few days.

By being a little more selective in the work commitments that he took, Don deliberately created more space in which to spend time writing. He had on several occasions worked with Howard Imber writing jokes and the occasional short sketch and script for television but had never seriously explored his potential as a serious writer. Mandy Rice-Davies had shared some of her own experiences of and ideas about writing and Don was encouraged to investigate his own skills in this realm. Some of his early attempts at short stories he sent off to women's magazines and was amazed when they were accepted for publication. One, entitled 'Rent a Sis', based on his own childhood experiences of being a lonely child, told of an only child who invents a big sister to brag about at school. Another tells of the exploits of a Welsh magician. These successes gave him the incentive to submit further scripts but it was his agent from Paul Vaughan Associates who first suggested that he should write for radio. Convinced that Don was a natural radio performer, he felt quite sure that he would know how to write for a listening audience. Not surprisingly the themes of his short stories were strongly linked to areas of personal interest. Flying, aircraft and the Second World War became settings for love stories, family feuds and daring escapades. Not only were six of Don's short stories accepted by BBC Radio 4's 'Morning Story' slot but he also became their reader.

Don had clearly got the writing bug, learning to carry with him wherever he went a small notebook in which he could jot down ideas and thoughts as they came into his head. The success of his short stories for radio gave him the confidence to think in terms of a novel. *Label of Love* was set against the background of the Six-Day War in Israel in 1967. It's a moving account of a mother who rediscovers the son who had been born to her in the new state of Israel in 1948. Their happy reunion is marred only by the onset of the Six-Day War. When he decides to return to Israel to fight she follows him. This moving love story became a screenplay and for several years a film company held rights to it. At one stage both Topol and Glenda Jackson read the script and expressed an interest in performing the lead parts. However, much to Don's sadness, it is a film yet to be made. *Like a Thunderbolt* is a second, unfinished novel, set in the slums of Birmingham at the beginning of the century and embracing the whole period of the First World War. Its story focuses on a brother and sister growing up in acute poverty, one turning to Catholicism, the other to Spiritualism. Many parts of the novel contain recognizable accounts and experiences from Don's own life and background, clearly written with feeling and empathy. He hopes to find time in the future to complete the near three-quarters written story and to see it published.

In amongst the breadth of work that Don was engaged in during these years he still maintained his commitment to the annual Christmas pantomime. By the end of the eighties, he had appeared in approximately twenty different productions since the start of his career and was emerging as one of the country's most experienced pantomime performers—also one of the most loved. Typically for Don, he was not content simply to repeat the same old material year after year but always looked for new and challenging ways of playing a character he may well have interpreted several times over. During these years he also moved into the writing and directing side of pantomime production. Researching local information to use on stage was nothing new to Don, or the daily input of topical jokes but the task of writing a complete script was yet another personal challenge that he tackled with enthusiasm and commitment. Wakefield, Guildford and Torquay were among the many towns to experience the writing and directing skills of Don Maclean but nowhere was more proud and appreciative than his home town of Birmingham. The production of *Aladdin* at the Old Rep Theatre remained special for a number of reasons. Having discovered that the city was to be without a traditional Christmas pantomime for the first time in many years, the *Birmingham Evening Mail* launched a major appeal to 'Save Our Panto'. The result was the first home-made panto for over fifteen years. Within the confines and restrictions of the tiny theatre it succeeded in providing a show of high-quality performance for families. The press raved about it with reviews such as:

This pantomime, written and directed by comedian Don Maclean, fizzes with fun and action. The jokes come fast and furious, many of them local and topical and the plot moves along at a smart pace, whisking us through changing moods and scenes. It's pantomime at its traditional best.

Acting, writing and directing had all served their purpose in filling the time gap left by television, as well as allowing Don to explore new territories within himself. Working men's clubs had not featured in his work schedule for some time but he continued to enjoy a number of regular cabaret engagements in some of the larger more up-market city night clubs. He appeared periodically at the New Cresta Club in Birmingham but this, along with many others of its kind closed down. These once popular night-time venues were being fast replaced by discos and bingo halls and an ever-increasing number of restaurants, leaving mounting unemployment amongst comedians. There was however a new market opening up that was becoming one of the few growth areas in the showbusiness industry for the alert and thinking performer. Don became the darling of this industry.

The world of corporate entertainment emerged as one of the most lucrative forms of employment open to top professional comedians in the mid- to late eighties and Don found himself in great demand. Large companies wanting to motivate their staff were no longer content with employing a comic to tell a few gags as a respite from the business side of a conference. Sales conferences were becoming as spectacular as West End musicals—and, in some cases, almost as expensive— with the entertainer featuring as an essential part of the cast. Some of the bigger organizations such as Ford, Abbey National and IBM laid to one side budgets of more than half a million pounds to set up their sales conventions, affording extravagant sets and expensive entertainers. Don remembers a conference where the stage became an enormous cardboard box from which leapt a dancing troupe. Another in Malta for Carlsberg, wheeled him on stage dressed in a wetsuit on a windsurfer in full sail against a background of fireworks. It is all aimed at generating enthusiasm and instilling a sense of team spirit and loyalty among workers and, on the whole, it appears to succeed. Don discovered the biggest spenders were car companies, who went to great lengths to ensure employees were excited about selling their latest models. To launch Ford's Orion, one design company took over Castle Ashby in Northampton and built a whole extension there. While guests were dining an entire wall was raised to reveal 50km (35 miles) of countryside in the centre of which hung an enormous moon-like screen. To the accompaniment of music composed specially for the evening and played by the London Symphony Orchestra, an Orion car was raised 6m (20 ft) in the air to the centre of the screen.

In just a short time Don's list of satisfied clients was beginning to read like a Who's Who in business, ranging from the Post Office to Cadbury's and from Smirnoff Vodka to SAAB and Leyland Trucks. What started as a small sideline in his increasingly varied list of engagements grew to occupy the majority of his work time and earned him more money than he had acquired in years. He was thoroughly enjoying it. Don took pride in researching every one of his corporate dates, taking seriously his responsibilities in getting to know the company and the people who worked for it. Consequently his material was always geared towards the individual and the issues that were of importance to both employer and employees. Prior to his performances he frequently attended company board meetings and chatted with management and workers, taking meticulous notes in preparation for his highly personalized material. He aimed to do a good job for each company concerned, knowing full well that no amount of advertising would attract work of this kind; it would come strictly from personal recommendation. Don's reputation escalated and he emerged in the top bracket of corporate entertainers in the country alongside the likes of Bob Monkhouse, Lance Percival and the late Roy Castle. His fame in the corporate world attracted wider media attention through a programme called 'Venture' made by Central Television which featured him in the first of a new series of business programmes aimed at taking a closer look at industries in the Midlands. It served a useful secondary purpose in keeping the wider public informed of his then most recent activities.

Although corporate work was beginning to dominate his time, Don wasn't by any means in danger of being removed from the wider, more public world of entertainment. Whilst not as many as he once would have liked, the opportunities for television and radio work still came his way and remained a smaller but nonetheless important part of his total work scene. Anglia's new game show 'Mouthtrap' received massive media coverage and looked likely, at one stage, to launch Don into the big time that he had recently come to terms with leaving behind. It was a light, loud and very raucous game show, of which he became the ideally suited energetic host. The competition among top comedians to present a game show was great and Don couldn't hide his delight at being asked by Anglia to become the programme's very first host.

'Mouthtrap' was new to Britain, based on an idea that had been adapted from an American show. After twenty-one years in the business Don was rarely lost for words and so it seemed appropriate that he should achieve his ambition of hosting a game show in which word association played a crucial part. He regularly informed the press that his greatest qualification for something called 'Mouthtrap' had to be his own mouth and teeth. They had become his most prominent feature during his five years working on 'Crackerjack' but he admits to not realizing just how the public had seen him until he started to receive a load of letters at that time about his mouth and teeth. The press homed in on the useful feature with headlines like 'Mac the Mouth', 'Mighty Mouth' and 'Don is in a Mouthtrap', all of which became an added attraction to the build-up of the show.

Anglia worked hard at promoting the show. They had experienced phenomenal success with 'Sale of the Century' a number of years earlier and were hopeful that 'Mouthtrap' would enjoy similar prosperity. However, it failed to attract the attention of the national network as they had hoped. It did well in both the Anglia and Granada regions where it had an evening slot but in other regions where it was screened in the afternoon, the audience ratings remained low. Don had enjoyed the strong team spirit that had come out of making 'Mouthtrap' and especially the chance to work with Howard Imber again but felt disappointed that a second series was not forthcoming. The team had given their all in making the best of what they eventually decided was an American idea that simply hadn't successfully crossed the ocean.

On occasions Don still took the initiative to create television and radio openings. It was Howard Imber who thought up the rather catchy title, 'Clever Dick-athlon', suggesting that it might make a good title for a comedy radio show. Don never needed asking twice and within a day or two had drawn up an outline for a quiz show, had approached the BBC about doing it and was ringing Howard to arrange to get together to start working together on some material. What emerged was a competition between three comedians aiming to outwit each other in ten gruelling events, each striving to become the Clever Dick of the week. The first in a series of six performances included Dave Lee, Bernie Clifton and Adrian Walsh and ran on Radio 2 for six consecutive Monday evenings. Once more Don proved the perfect questionmaster and went on to make several more series for well-satisfied BBC producer Andy Aliffe.

The diversity of work that Don took on during the mid- to late eighties brought with it a varied lifestyle ranging from hours upon hours of quiet research and writing to racing from one end of the country to the other in order to serve the corporate market. It suited his adaptable and high-energy personality and he clearly thrived on the many different challenges and experiences offered in the process. He felt privileged to be able to explore new territories within himself and his profession and yet still enjoy what he was both experienced and good at. There were no regrets about his decision not to strive for the top, as he was finding life both extremely busy and fulfilling. But in amongst the business he never failed to allow time for personal pleasure and enjoyment.

12

Work Hard, Play Hard

Don has always believed in living life to the full. Whether working, being with the family or simply pursuing his personal interests and hobbies, he gives of his all, sets high standards and strives always to reach his potential. He works in order to succeed and plays in order to win. There is hardly an area of his life which doesn't reflect his hard-working, determined and yet fun-loving personality. Whilst there are things of interest and importance to pursue he sees little point in losing valuable waking hours, so he reluctantly succumbs to the minimal amount of sleep that his body requires. The line dividing work and leisure is very finely drawn as he has always found great joy and delight in pursuing both and, on many occasions, they have come together in the most fulfilling way. His 'work hard, play hard' philosophy speaks not so much of the division of time between two worlds but more of the pursuit of both excellence and enjoyment in both.

Don must be one of the most consistent people alive. Unlike so many others in the world of entertainment, who have allowed the pressures and privileges of their lifestyle to change them, he has remained constant in his personality, retaining and developing virtually all the interests and hobbies that he pursued as a child. The boy who displayed a spirit of fierce competition on the sports field and a childhood obsession with aeroplanes is clearly identifiable in the man. Over thirty years on, no one from either Sparkbrook Primary or St Philip's Grammar School would be surprised to hear of his continued sporting talent or his competence as a pilot.

He has always enjoyed good health and has felt it important to retain a high level of fitness, in view of the hectic pace of his life. The erratic work schedule has always made it difficult for him to be part of a soccer, rugby or athletics squad that he so enjoyed in his youth, consequently, when he noticed his body weight slowly increasing, he looked for a form of exercise that he could pursue in a variety of places and at different times. Don discovered squash—or, as it sometimes appears, squash discovered Don! His only regret is that it took him over thirty years of his life to come into contact with what he considers the finest game ever invented.

During his search friends had suggested various other sports, including golf which clearly surfaces as the most popular form of relaxation among showbiz personalities. The thought of spending several hundreds of pounds a year in order to hit a ball and then walk after it seemed quite ridiculous to Don. 'If you want it bad enough to walk after it, why hit it in the first place?' he regularly asked golfers, adding, 'In squash at least the ball comes back to you.'

This new discovery fitted perfectly into his lifestyle. With the Solihull Arden Club virtually backing on to his house, he had no difficulty when at home in finding a partner or receiving regular coaching in the early stages of his mastering the sport. Within a short time, he had earned himself a place in the squad competing in local club leagues. This fuelled his competitive spirit and made him even more determined to improve his standard. When travelling he found few difficulties in finding a court or a partner, with many of the clubs in the London area making him a honorary member. Squash became an addiction and, within just a few years of learning the game, Don was playing in the Solihull Arden first team and as Number 3 in the Heathrow first team. The former Warwickshire County teenage half miler had clearly not lost his speed, his natural sporting skill or the will to win.

Squash has become Don's most serious long-term pursuit since he embarked upon the world of show business. Having quickly achieved a high standard, he looked further afield for top-level coaching and competitive play. The former RAF physical training instructor and fitness expert, Brian 'Bomber' Harris, who coached many of the country's top players including one-time world champion Jonah Barrington, took Don to the peaks of fitness, which prepared him for his loftiest ambition. The best thing for him about reaching forty-five years of age was his qualification to compete for a place as a veteran in the Warwickshire county veteran squad. By this time he had already scooped the title of British Celebrity Champion, beating both the late Leonard Rossiter and Tommy Steele who had held the title for a number of years previously. Don's high level of fitness, his fierce competitive streak and sheer determination won him the long-coveted accolade of representing his county at the age of forty-six.

The world of squash took full advantage of the skills and talents of their most well-known recruit, inviting him to appear and perform on and off court in a wide range of social and publicity events. Don was once more only too pleased to combine his professional and leisure worlds, especially when the occasions benefited local and national charities. He developed a popular routine on court with some of the country's finest players, offering demonstration games for public viewing. He even managed a couple of friendly games with Jonah Barrington himself, following which he gave a frequently-recounted interview with sports presenter Gary Newbon. It went like this:

Newbon: 'I hear you play the odd game with Jonah, Don?'

Maclean: 'Yes, but not any more.'

Newbon: 'Why not?'

Maclean: 'Would you play with somebody who picks up the ball on the second bounce, calls your serves out when they're in and fiddles the score?'

Newbon: 'I certainly wouldn't.'

Maclean: 'Well, neither would Jonah!'

Don delighted in becoming known as the person to bring humour into the game. One of the major squash journals invited him to write several short humorous pieces for monthly publication. Little did he realize when agreeing to do so that he would end up writing an entire book. *Maclean Up Squash* was first published in 1982, providing a popular and hilarious view of the game and its players. Selling 15,000 copies, its short stories (largely fictitious), spicy anecdotes, accounts of dressing-room conversations and the inevitable list of Maclean jokes and tips has entertained many who share his passion for the game. The book attracted a lot of media interest—though nowhere near as much as when he decided to take out an insurance policy against damage incurred to his teeth on court. He regularly informed journalists, 'My toothy grin has become a trademark and I've seen many players take the full force of a racket in the mouth. I can't afford to be without my teeth so the policy seemed the logical step.' Fortunately he has never had cause to cash in on his investment.

Don's other major leisure interest also finds its roots in his childhood, in the days when, as a very small boy, he was taken by his father to the R.A.F. station at Castle Bromwich Airfield, an important war-time base. (It now accommodates literally hundreds of high-rise flats and houses, known as the Castle Vale

Estate.) In the post-war years there was an annual open day when the general public were permitted to look round the base and watch a flying display of some of the finest aircraft used during the war. The famous Spitfire was built there and Don recalls desperately wanting to climb into the cockpit and imagine himself as a pilot. Simply standing close by these magnificent flying machines fuelled his imagination with the dream of one day flying his own plane. Whilst at St Philip's he had wanted to join the Air Training Corps, in the hope of turning his dream into reality but the staff decided that the demands of his academic studies were to be given a higher priority. For a while Don put his dreams of flying to one side.

Many years later in 1984, during a summer season at Clacton he found himself with spare time on his hands. It was one of the few summer seasons that he had agreed to take on during the children's teenage years and coincided with Rachel's G.C.E. examinations. Unusually, Don had gone ahead of the family to work the first few weeks of the season without them. Following rehearsals one day he took himself off to the local airfield to watch the small private planes fly in and out. Whilst there, one of the resident airport staff asked him if he had ever considered taking flying lessons. Don delighted in sharing with him his childhood dreams and fascination with war-time aviation. It didn't take long for the chief flying instructor, Eric Shipley, to persuade him to consider seriously the idea of enrolling on one of their intensive courses that guaranteed a pilot's licence at the end. Eighteen hundred pounds in order to pursue a hobby felt expensive but when Don realized that the cost included full accommodation, meals, instruction and examination fees he was tempted. Having talked it over with Toni, he returned the following day to negotiate a package that would fit in with his summer season routine. For the next five weeks he took a lesson each morning and afternoon, followed by ground-school instruction in preparation for three written PPL examinations. It fulfilled his wildest dreams when, after just eleven hours' instruction in the air, he made his first solo flight. The experience was both exhilarating and terrifying. He followed the exact routine completed many times over with his instructor—except for one minor detail. Having successfully taken off, turned left and flown down wind he was expected to radio into control with his call sign, 'Romeo Oscar'. Don was literally on cloud nine, ecstatically absorbed in the whole experience and unable to restrain the compulsion to sing out loud. Remembering to contact control, he announced to the world, 'Romeo Oscar, down wind, singing "Amazing Grace".' It was the first of many solo flights but the one that will always remain a most special moment in his life. He celebrated back on the ground with strawberries and cream. Having successfully passed all the official written papers, he was later presented with his private pilot's licence.

Don loves flying simply for flying's sake. He finds it relaxing and totally absorbing, leaving him unable to think about anything else. The geography is irrelevant except, of course, when he is able to use the plane as a personal mode of transport to and from various work commitments in different parts of the country. At first he hired an aircraft each time he wanted to fly, feeling reluctant to incur the expense of buying one but as time went on realized that in order to maintain his confidence and keep up his flying expertise it made far more sense to purchase his own. He became the proud owner of a two-seater Piper Tomahawk, which he decided to make available to other pilots, in order to help with costs. Sadly, it was crashed less than a year later. It was a painful parting for Don and caused him to review his decision to hire it out for use by others. Ten years and two planes later he now owns a four-seater Grumman Tiger (G-DON1) and engages in over one hundred hours of flying a year. It's a mixture of work and pleasure but few things cause him to relax and enjoy himself more than being able to enjoy the total freedom he experiences when flying.

Don's love of flying is intrinsically linked with his fascination with First World War history. The roots of this interest also reach back many years. When working on the Isle of Sheppey in one of his first holiday camps, he walked each Sunday morning to the Catholic church in Sheerness for the 11a.m. mass. Halfway up the church on one side was a Royal Flying Corps cap badge, underneath which hung a plaque dedicated to three members of the same family, all of whom had lost their lives in active service during the First World War. William, James and Anthony Macudden held a whole host of decorations between them. The young men's lives intrigued Don so much that he decided to investigate their stories in more detail.

The further he delved, the more fascinated he became by their lives and the circumstances that caused their deaths. Don describes the impact of this discovery as like the opening of Aladdin's cave. He had entered into a world of aviation and war history that has since become a passion and a delight, governing many happy hours of leisure reading. Shelves of books line the walls of his study, over fifty watercolours cover the walls of his lounge with many more oil and pen-and-ink pictures of pre-1919 aircraft. Scattered throughout the house is an amazing collection of First World War memorabilia: photographs, model aircraft and oddities such as the end of a propeller and some hand-painted RAF wings. All of this stemmed from the reading of one memorial plaque on the wall of a small church when he was just nineteen years of age.

In his mid-forties, Don's pursuit of historical knowledge took a further unexpected turn. The Solihull College of Technology, close by his home, invited him to officiate at the opening of their newly built extension. Happy to do whatever he could in the local community, Don accepted the invitation. Following the official cutting of a ribbon and the subsequent speeches, he was taken on a guided tour of various departments by one of the senior lecturers, who also happened to

be a fellow worshipper at Don's home church. Colette Ware
noted his interest in the history room and, in the course of
conversation, suggested that he signed up to study part-time for
an 'A' level in modern/political history. At first he thought the
idea beyond his capabilities—he had not studied since he was
sixteen years of age—not to mention impractical with his work
commitments. But Colette convinced him otherwise. For as
many weeks as he was able, Don attended the three-hour
history classes each Thursday evening. In just one academic
year he had completed the syllabus and attained an A grade in
'A' level history. He was truly delighted with his achievements.
Not only had he increased his knowledge of history beyond the
self-taught period of the First World War but he had also
achieved an impressive qualification into the bargain. Colette
Ware clearly recognized the potential of her new student and
wasted no time in suggesting that Don continued his studies by
taking a degree course at Warwick University. This time Don
really did think she was joking but once more she proved it
possible within the limitations of his work. Initially Warwick
University students were intrigued by the presence of a comedy
entertainer in their midst but soon realized the extent of his
knowledge and motivation to study. They quickly accepted him
as simply another student, even when on odd occasions he
would appear dressed in bow tie and dinner jacket, ready to
dash off to do an after-dinner speech or cabaret booking. Don's
degree course is on-going; he has completed half the number of
modules required for degree status. The flexibility of the part-
time course allows him the vital extended breaks when his work
commitments prevent him from spending the necessary
amount of time both studying and attending lectures.

The Birmingham media delighted in his academic success
and his use of the city's adult education facilities. Birmingham
people had long since claimed Don as their very own and the
feelings of ownership is evidently mutual. Known to most as the
centre of the country and the heart of the Midlands, Birmingham

remains no less than the hub of the nation for Don Maclean. It has been his home for over fifty years and he has never wanted to live anywhere else. He is fascinated by its history and development, proud of its achievements and holds great affection for many of its fine landmarks and surrounding countryside. Most of all he loves the people. He is one of them.

Naturally Birmingham's own history has been a topic high on Don's reading list for many years. The growth of a once small village which stood on the outskirts of Aston town into what has been described as 'the first manufacturing town in the world' intrigues him. Everything he has ever read and learned about the city's growth and development appears positive and constructive to him. Certain aspects fascinate him. The fact that once every gilt button sewn onto military uniforms all over the world was made in his home city fills him with immense pride. Other flourishing cottage industries of the eighteenth century based upon the skills and creativity of the city's handicraft workers—jewellery, toys and guns— makes him proud to be one of their descendants. During the booming years of the Industrial Revolution, many of the industrial entrepreneurs of the eighteenth century gravitated towards Birmingham. Some were natives of the city whilst others made it their home as a result of their pioneering work there. Men such as Joseph Priestley, James Brindley, William Hutton, John Taylor, Matthew Boulton, James Watt and Thomas Telford clearly recognized the importance of its central location and creative workforce as each made their mark upon the rapidly growing Midlands town. Few other leading cities in Britain can boast quite such a long list of influential inventors and entrepreneurs in their history books. Don Maclean is never slow to share in that boasting process, making known the historical wealth and resources of the city to any audience that is prepared to listen.

Many of the historical buildings of the relatively young city of Birmingham remain important landmarks for Don. To him they are magnificent structures, full of richness and culture. The early architects responsible for the town hall, city squares and railway stations based their designs on Roman and Greek architecture. Such early designs were clearly recognized as marks of civilization and grandeur, both of which the first designers felt Birmingham was worthy of displaying. The splendid Roman Catholic Oratory is for Don a step into Rome itself.

He remains convinced that those who criticize and ridicule Birmingham are those who have never visited the city. In all his travels he feels sure that this city centre is one of the safest in the country. The beautifully restored Centenary and Victoria Squares provide central meeting points in which Birmingham's people can gather. The blend of old and new has been skilfully and tastefully combined, creating an environment which reflects the best of past achievements and yet looks forward positively to the future. Don loves taking part in outside broadcasts of any kind but especially when they make use of his home town. In recent years the city squares have hosted a number of special television and radio broadcasts in which he has been delighted to participate. The fact that Birmingham has three theatres, two concert halls, is home to a leading national orchestra and royal ballet company and is the location for the expansive National Exhibition Centre must make it, in Don's 'unbiased' opinion, one of the finest, most creative and resourceful cities in our country.

Understandably Don defends his home town from all critics, recognizing that the view most passers by gain is of large industrial chimney stacks or the motorway network of Spaghetti Junction. Few venture further to discover the many oases of green both within and surrounding the city itself. Many of the city's leading manufacturers were concerned to maintain a greenbelt area that was accessible and enjoyable to its workers and residents. The well-known chocolate manufacturer Cadbury's gave much of this land to the people. Such foresight has provided Birmingham with rich and pleasant countryside for many years. The famous Lickey Hills were only a tram ride away to those living centrally and were a regular Sunday and Bank Holiday visiting spot for Don and his family when he was a child. Many of the parks were also developed and maintained by the manufacturing companies, who took great interest in the social needs of their workforces. A deep paternal concern for the people emerged and is clearly still in evidence today. Don's own 'work hard, play hard' philosophy was shared by both employers and employees of Birmingham and benefited the whole community. Today, with its extensive motorway network, good public transport systems and the increase in private car ownership beautiful, green surroundings can be reached within a short travelling time. Don is the first to recognize and enjoy these benefits.

In the latter part of this century the 'city of a thousand trades' has attracted large numbers of unemployed people from all over the country. It also became one of the first areas to receive immigrants in search of work and housing. Asian families in particular gravitated towards the city and especially the Sparkbrook area in which Don grew up. The changes in culture, lifestyle, language and religion don't trouble him or remove his fond memories of the years spent here. If anything it reflects for him the unique diversity of the group of people who call themselves 'Brummies'. Qualification is by birth—or adoption as Don's father had discovered for himself many years before. Birmingham has learned to receive people and welcome them as part of its diverse and yet united identity. Few barriers exist and Don is firmly convinced that the people have emerged as a warm-hearted, down-to-earth, caring community.

Don Maclean must be one of Birmingham's greatest ambassadors. He never misses an opportunity to promote his home town and people and gives inexhaustibly of his time and energy to as many charitable causes as he can. He holds a particular affection for organizations that support work with children, especially those with physical and mental disability or terminal illness. He happily participates in activities and events set up to raise money, doing all he can to encourage others to play their part too. Over the years he has walked, run, cycled, swum, flown and taken part in numerous games of football, rugby—and, of course, squash—in aid of one good cause or another. He is patron of the Acorns Children's Hospice in Birmingham and has shared for many years in the work of an organization called the Across Trust who help disabled adults and children to take holidays abroad. Don struggles to understand why so many children have to suffer but strives in his confusion to bring what he sees as his small offering to brighten their lives. Few children fail to respond to his boyish charm and humour and he helps many more parents find strength to smile in the midst of the pain of watching their young ones suffer. Nor is Don's work for charity restricted to the realms of Birmingham; whenever working away for any length of time he tries hard to responds to the many local invitations that come his way.

Where charity work is concerned, perhaps his greatest privilege of all has come in more recent years through working with the BBC 'Children in Need' appeal. He considers it an honour to employ all of his professional skills in work that he both loves and which at the same time can offer so much good. For three consecutive years Don has travelled the country with the Radio 2 crew, calling in on a wide range of people's extraordinary fund-raising efforts. His depth and sincerity as a person combined with his fun-loving, energetic personality make him the perfect choice for such an important role.

13

The James Whale
Radio Show

Live cabaret work remained a small but ongoing part of Don's work schedule throughout the eighties, often taking him to a number of different venues and parts of the country. Among his favourites is the Leeds City Varieties, a small, traditional theatre famous for its filming of the BBC's 'The Good Old Days' and extremely popular among many artists. It was whilst working there in April 1990 that Don received a somewhat unusual last-minute invitation to take part in a live discussion on a late-night show produced by the then Yorkshire Television Company. The fact that it was last-minute wasn't unusual in itself; it was more the style of the show that took him by surprise. It turned out to be quite different from anything that he had ever done before.

The 'difference' started in the title: 'The James Whale Radio Show' was in fact a television programme. Mr Whale himself first gained notoriety as a radio disc jockey whose late night/early morning phone-in programmes attracted enormous public response, achieving very high audience ratings. He tackled numerous subjects, many topical and controversial whilst others were simply bizarre. He quickly gained a reputation for being an assertive, aggressive and argumentative presenter with the skill to entice equally contentious reactions from his listeners. At its peak the programme developed a following of almost cult proportions, particularly among the young. Such was its success that Yorkshire Television invited him and his programme onto the television screen, not as a comfortable chat show with couches and soft lights but the literal filming of a live phone-in radio broadcast incorporating discussion from an invited panel of guests. It was one particular programme in this televised series that Don was asked to take part in although he knew nothing about either the programme or the presenter.

The invitation was quite specific. Don was informed that the subject to be discussed was 'religion' and his role was to defend Roman Catholicism. That particular night the panel consisted of three men; himself, the Methodist minister Frank Topping and a convert to the Muslim faith and founder of an Islamic political party. Apart from the occasional appearance at special services for the Catholic Stage Guild, this was the first time Don had ever been asked to represent his religion and he was delighted to be able to do so.

Prior to the programme, members of the studio panel met informally with James Whale, enjoying pleasant conversation and a drink. His hospitality was warm and generous and Don felt confident that they were in for an interesting and stimulating discussion. What he hadn't banked on was the seeming transformation of personality that Mr Whale underwent as he walked from the hospitality suite into the studio. The charming, warm and friendly host became a rather loud and aggressive bully clearly determined to find a way in which he could question, challenge, or provoke anyone who had anything to say on the chosen subject. Don, who is rarely lost for words, was, on this occasion, very grateful that he wasn't first in the firing line. The so-called 'discussion' became a James Whale monologue interspersed with an occasional comment from a caller or panel member when invited to do so by Mr Whale. Within the opening minutes of the discussion neither Frank Topping (the only panel member, at this stage, granted permission to speak) or any of the phone-in guests had succeeded in completing a single sentence without being cut off, rudely interrupted or simply told to 'shut up' in several different forms. Don had the distinct advantage of a minute or two in which to assess the situation and gather his initial thoughts together. It became clear that everyone in and outside the studio was under attack and he knew that he had to decide upon his line of defence. His turn came round all too soon.

Despite being initially complimented by James Whale as one of the few people in entertainment willing to identify himself as religious (this was quickly followed by a tongue in cheek reference to the fact that Cliff Richard was unavailable) Don knew he had to draw upon his every skill as a comedian and broadcaster. Momentarily he turned the whole show into a comic game; in reply to every comment or question directed at him he produced a wisecrack. It wasn't that he was reluctant to speak out about his faith, simply that he wasn't prepared to allow what he had to say about God and Catholicism to be ridiculed and mocked in such an aggressive manner. As a result, James Whale threw every conceivable criticism and insult about Catholicism that he could think of at Don who successfully fielded each one of them with short, sharp, witty responses. The production team loved every minute of it and their muffled laughter could be clearly heard in the background. The viewers' interest and sympathy was quickly turning away from the presenter and towards Don. One caller even phoned in specifically to say hello to Don and express how nice it was to see him back on television after so many years. For the next few minutes the programme was in danger of becoming 'The Don Maclean Show'. Don's plan had worked and he was successfully demonstrating to Mr Whale that there was at least one person in the studio who could think fast on his feet and would not easily be put down. Despite the fact that Don didn't like this man's style of interviewing or agree with his approach to the subject in hand, he had to acknowledge and admire his obvious skills in broadcasting. His brain worked fast and his mouth even faster—but he was clearly finding Don a challenge. Accusing him directly of going off the point (which Don was deliberately doing) James Whale began to show exasperation at not being able to extract one serious comment from him about his faith or church.

The strategy worked well for a while until one caller raised a topic that Don just could not pass off with a joke. The subject hit a raw nerve and he suddenly found himself passionately defending his faith. The issue at stake concerned the raising of children in the Roman Catholic faith. The caller explained that he was not a Catholic although his wife was and he objected to having to agree to have children baptized and raised in the Roman Catholic Church. His preference would have been for both children to be allowed to decide upon a faith for them-selves at a later stage of their life. James Whale thought it a fair comment but, before he had managed to add his opinions, Don interrupted with his own very strong feelings on the subject. 'That's utter nonsense' he declared. 'You've got to give a child something before he or she can choose—otherwise they have no choice.' The spark grew quickly into a flame. Don persisted with the argument, explaining that many may wish to change their denomination or even religion at a later stage in life but everyone needs some kind of foundation and beginning to faith.

He quickly drew upon the experiences of the other two guests present both of whom had started out in life as Roman Catholics. One had changed religion completely and converted to the Muslim faith whilst Frank Topping had come out of Catholicism and, later in life, had become a Methodist. Don left the viewers in no doubt of the fact that, in his personal opinion, he had benefited from the very best decision of all, in both starting and continuing in life as a Catholic! He spoke for no more than fifteen to twenty seconds but was the only panel member, up to that point, to succeed in completing what he'd wanted to say. Don Maclean had made himself heard.

The programme continued for a while in its bizarre style of aborted discussion between presenter, caller and panel but Don had definitely moved into a different gear. Having successfully been heard once, he abandoned his original strategy and waited patiently for the next opportunity to defend the faith. The presenter himself opened up the way for him this time. Having been asked by a caller if he actually believed in God, James Whale made a very reluctant confession that he did. He was very obviously and unusually embarrassed by this positive response and followed it with an immediate expression of regret as to having admitted what might be considered by some viewers as a chink in his steely-armoured image. He actually went on to say that he was fearful of losing his credibility with the audience through such a public statement.

Don was visibly amazed by this comment. He failed to grasp why admitting a belief in God should cause anyone to lose their credibility. For him it was the reverse. He successfully launched into his second very convincing speech of the evening—or early morning as it was by that time—explaining how atheists, in his opinion, are the bravest people alive. He continued:

> *To actually believe that there is no more to life than simply the here and now and that what we do in life is unimportant or of no greater long-term purpose or that we won't be called to account for the things that we've done, takes far more courage than I have got.*

On this occasion there was almost a murmur of agreement from James Whale, along with a sense of relief as he recognized that Don's words had actually rescued him from an unexpected moment of floundering and helped reinstate him before the audience. The mood of the conversation changed momentarily from one of flippancy to sincerity. Don took full advantage of the shift and went on to say how publicly identifying himself as a Christian and especially as a Roman Catholic was a strength and something he was extremely proud of. The message was coming across loud and clear and the more he spoke the stronger it became. Don Maclean was clearly emerging as a great ambassador of the Christian faith and the Roman Catholic Church.

One person watching the James Whale Radio Show that night was a producer working for BBC Religious Broadcasting. Michael Wakelin was senior producer for Radio 2's 'Good Morning Sunday', a one-and-a-half-hour weekly programme that had enjoyed nearly ten years of success on the religious broadcasting scene. The show's presenter for the previous five years had been the well-known broadcaster and Anglican priest Roger Royle who had, several months earlier, given considerable advance notice of his decision to leave in order to take up a new position as chaplain at the Lord Mayor Trelawe College for people with severe mental disabilities in Hampshire. His resignation had been received with sadness by all who had worked with him and tuned into the programme. Roger was a gracious, loving man with a good sense of humour, much loved by his million or more listeners. The production team knew that he would be difficult to replace and the task of appointing his successor lay chiefly with Michael Wakelin and the Rev. Ernest Rea, Head of BBC Religious Broadcasting.

One of the first people to be seriously considered for the position was the late Roy Castle who had regularly stood in on 'Good Morning Sunday' when Roger was on holiday. The listeners had always enjoyed Roy's lively personality, love of music and sincere faith and Michael knew that he would be an able successor to Roger. Roy would have loved to have taken on the show but was heavily engaged in recording the successful 'Record Breakers' series which absorbed large chunks of his working week. He was also undergoing tests for a then un-diagnosed illness so thought it unwise to over-commit him-self. The production team were disappointed, as Roy Castle would have fitted their bill perfectly: someone who successfully combined both showbusiness appeal and religious faith.

There were two schools of thought about the future. The BBC knew that they could appoint someone similar to Roger, who could do a good, professional and 'safe' job, satisfying the religious listening constituency. Or they could take a risk and go for someone with a completely different style. The blend of show business and religion appealed to both Michael Wakelin and Ernie Rea but the task of finding the right person was clearly not going to be easy. They were looking for the kind of presenter who would make the audience sit up and listen, perhaps say and do surprising things and generally fit easily into the whole ethos of Radio 2. It was easier said than done.

After much deliberation a decision was made to draw up a short-list of four different presenters of varying styles. Each were offered three weeks in which to present the show over the summer months of 1990, after which they hoped to be able to offer the most suitable candidate a permanent contract. All four selected had been associated with broadcasting in one way or another.

The Irish singer Dana was the only woman in the group. Well known for her strong Christian beliefs and Roman Catholic identity, she clearly fitted into the category of a big showbusiness personality. Ian Gall was familiar to some, having already presented 'Songs of Praise' on several occasions. Michael Wakelin knew that he could be an exceptionally funny man and hoped that he might bring his own individual type of humour to the programme. Both Colin Semper and Frank Topping had featured strongly in the religious broadcasting scene for many years and were experienced as well as fairly 'safe' prospects. In order to bring some continuity into this trial period, the production team launched a competition to find the listeners' top ten favourite hymns. A number of famous personalities also added their own choices, through specially pre-recorded interviews. The idea caught on well with thousands of listeners writing in giving the reasons for their personal favourites. It successfully held together what might have otherwise been a very disjointed period in the life of 'Good Morning Sunday'.

Don Maclean was not part of the original line-up of names to be considered for the presenter's job. In fact he was an unknown name in the world of religious broadcasting. Some in the department had vague recollections of him in 'Crackerjack' and the Black and White Minstrels but had heard very little of him since those days. Michael himself knew nothing at all about the man other than what he had seen and heard on 'The James Whale Radio Show' that night. He simply had a gut feeling that Don Maclean could become the very different kind of presenter that they were looking for and set about the task of unearthing as much as he could about him. The discovery, only days later, of Don's many years of experience with Radio 2 through the Light Entertainment Department simply fuelled that conviction. Ernie Rea shared his enthusiasm, agreeing that Don should be offered the chance of a three-week trial with the original line-up of the four others.

Don knew nothing of the BBC's enquiry until he returned from a week working for a computer company in Athens. As always, he phoned his agent in order to check on his work schedule, only to discover that the BBC had been eagerly awaiting his return in order to arrange a meeting at the earliest opportunity to talk about the possibility of him presenting the Sunday morning programme. At first he thought it a huge joke and when he told Toni she laughed too. He had never imagined himself as a religious broadcaster and the idea took some getting used to but he nonetheless agreed to meet up with Ernie Rea along with Michael Wakelin and several other members of the production team.

Don had listened to the programme sufficiently to know that Roger Royle was a deeply spiritual man with the skills and capacity to befriend a large number of people through the show. He was a wonderful priest, pastor and friend to all who listened. The contrast between the two men was extreme and Don wasn't convinced that this was a job to which he was at all suited. Throughout the meeting, over an Indian meal, Don listened and asked questions and confesses to spending most of the time with his tongue in his cheek, playing devil's advocate. He remembers Michael Wakelin being very intense and nervous about the occasion. Don couldn't resist the temptation to wind him up a little, by finding something funny in almost everything he said. Michael battled on doing most of the talking; one minute telling Don that he had all that they were looking for in a new presenter and yet in the next breath warning him that it wasn't a comedy show and he wouldn't be able to tell numerous jokes. He emphasized the fact that Don would be required to be sensitive to other faiths and denominations and just how important it would be for him not to overstate his Catholicism and run the risk of ostracizing non-Catholic listeners. (Don found that he wanted to laugh, after all, telling jokes and being Catholic just about summed up him as a person.) In effect he had to realize that he would become the main spokesman for religious broadcasting on Radio 2 and the only contact that many listeners have with 'religion' all week. It was a huge responsibility and as the meal progressed he became less and less sure that this was the right job for him, nevertheless, he agreed to a trial period of three weeks.

The following Sunday Don and Toni set the alarm for 7.30a.m. and listened to every minute of the one-and-a-half-hour show in silence. They were full of admiration for Roger Royle, appreciative of his gifts and his style in presenting but Don knew that he couldn't even get close to being like him. At the end of the ninety-minute programme Toni confirmed his feelings by simply saying, 'This is not for you.' However, having committed himself to the three weeks he accepted the challenge and set about the task of preparing as well as he could.

The first went out in July as Don took over the hot seat from the soft-voiced and gentle-spirited Dana. The contrast between the two probably couldn't have been greater as he left listeners in no doubt as to the fact that there had been a change. 'Good morning, good morning, good morning Sunday,' announced the unmistakable voice of the Birmingham comic. 'This is Don Maclean with you for three weeks. That's not three weeks in one lump—just ninety minutes to start with! Speaking of starting, isn't it a beautiful morning—would you like a record to commemorate that fact? Here's Howard Keele, singing "O what a beautiful morning" ' His opening words came out fast and furiously light-hearted, clearly revealing the bounce and vibrancy of his personality. Don had made his mark right from the start in simply being himself. The mould had been well and truly cracked. By nature of temperament he couldn't avoid integrating a few laughs into the programme—not to have done so would have denied him his own identity and that was something he had no intention of sacrificing for any job. He had decided before agreeing to the trial that either the Religious Broadcasting Department would accept him for who and what he was or he would happily walk away. Whatever the long-term outcome he felt he had nothing to lose. He intended to enjoy it.

Don brought to 'Good Morning Sunday' many years of experience in radio broadcasting, the fruit of which gave him considerable confidence in hosting a live show although there were certain aspects of this particular job that were completely new. The production team were very supportive and encouraging and welcomed his own comments and contribution. Quite early on in discussions he had expressed surprise at the fact that the programme had never included prayer. The comment was quickly picked up and Don became the first presenter to write and read his own prayers for ninety seconds of the programme time. He quickly learned to scour the newspapers and religious current affairs scene in order to write his prayers based on the bidding prayers he had been bred on in the Roman Catholic Church. They were well received and helped him to feel that he had made a personal contribution towards the content of his first programme.

One long standing feature of 'Good Morning Sunday' was the special guest interviews that took place weekly at around 8.20a.m., the time at which the number of listeners reached its peak. Don had never conducted an interview of any kind, least of all one that was likely to deal with spiritual matters. He wasn't afraid to ask for advice and the production team were very keen to help. His very first guest was the Governor of the Bank of England—Robin Lee Pemberton. Don admits to knowing virtually nothing about the man or his job and was unusually anxious about the whole thing. He prepared thoroughly with the help of his researcher, Rosemary Foxcroft. On this occasion the interview was scheduled to be pre-recorded which allowed time for some editing to take place if things didn't go smoothly.

When the time came, Michael Wakelin confessed to being more nervous than Don as it was his own head on the block if things went wrong. There was no doubt that Don had been taken on board on the strength on Michael's personal convictions and so it was important to him that the whole programme, especially the interview, went well. On hearing Don's opening line he had his doubts. Once more the unmistakable Brummie voice declared, 'Good morning Guv'na— do people actually call you "Guv'na"?' Don had instinctively tried to get a laugh but it didn't quite come off. The interview got off to a rough start but gradually both Don and his guest became more relaxed and the end result, after editing, was just about acceptable to the production team. Immediately following the Sunday broadcast Don rang Toni and was surprised by her response. Despite the struggle with the interview and one or two minor hiccups, she admitted to Don that she was beginning to think that perhaps it was something he would be good at after all.

There was a gap of several weeks between the first and subsequent two programmes that Don was to due to present. During this time his mother's health deteriorated considerably. She had been suffering with Alzheimer's disease for over five years and was becoming increasingly confused and disorientated. Since she was living in a nursing home just around the corner from his Solihull home, Don was able to call in to see her every day. Following a bad fall she broke her leg and was admitted to hospital, where she deteriorated rapidly, eventually contracting pleurisy. Rosie Maclean died shortly afterwards on Tuesday 18 September 1990.

Don presented 'Good Morning Sunday' throughout this difficult period of his life. Instead of burying his emotion and putting on a brave face to his listeners he courageously talked about his mother, her illness and how he was coping with her death. His comments touched large numbers of listeners, who wrote in both to thank him for sharing his grief and to offer words of comfort and encouragement. He had obviously struck a chord within many of his listeners' lives and the impact of that did not go unnoticed by the production team.

Don had thoroughly enjoyed his trial with 'Good Morning Sunday'. It had challenged and stretched him in yet another direction in his ever-expanding career. Contrary to what he had first imagined, he now felt quite strongly about wanting to become the programme's next presenter. His competitive spirit had resurfaced and he was prepared to put all his energies into ensuring that he was the BBC's first choice among the five contenders. He knew that it would change his life quite considerably, not least in respect of his attendance at mass each Sunday. Accompanying his two children each week had been a very high priority, one he was reluctant to let go. However, Don had no doubt in his mind that, should he be offered the position, he would accept it willingly.

14

'Good Morning Sunday'

'Good Morning Sunday' has become one of the big success stories of religious broadcasting. Its aim—to reach a wide popular audience with top-quality religious programmes—was established early on in its fifteen-year history. During the mid-eighties it became one of the first religious programmes of its kind to attain the one million listeners mark, giving great cause for celebration within the whole religious broadcasting department. Producers, researchers and presenters have changed but all have continued both to sustain the interest and popularity of the programme and to increase the audience ratings. In the last five years there has been an extraordinary leap in figures, achieving new and unbeaten records. In 1995 'Good Morning Sunday' reached an audience of two million people. Not only does it continue to produce the highest ratings of all programmes on religious radio broadcasting (beaten only, within the total religious broadcasting network by BBC television's 'Songs of Praise') but it also attracts the largest audience of all Radio 2 programmes broadcast on a Sunday. This exceptional increase has come about since 1990 and is largely attributed to the popularity of Don Maclean as the show's new presenter.

Appointing Don as presenter of 'Good Morning Sunday' was, in the words of the Head of Religious Broadcasting, 'a high-risk strategy'. Don's style was completely different from the safe and secure approach adopted by his predecessor. Never before had the BBC employed a comedian and entertainer to take up what had become a very established, conservative role. The producers knew that there would be an audience reaction and also realized some of the potential dangers of such a radical decision but, in terms of contemporary religious broadcasting, the possibilities were both great and exciting. The production team invited and welcomed the change and looked forward to the challenges that it would present.

Michael Wakelin and Ernie Rea never had any serious doubts about Don's ability to present the show. They remained united in the conviction that here was a man with the necessary professional skills, strong religious convictions and quality of personality to communicate positive thinking about God and religion effectively across the air waves. The underlying philosophy of 'Good Morning Sunday' is to make faith, especially Christianity, a very natural, accessible and important part of ordinary life—not the restricted and exclusive right of clergy or even of regular church-goers. It is a task made all the more challenging in the light of the prevailing climate of British society which has fast developed the attitude that religion and faith are both irrelevant and outdated.

A recent survey conducted by the BBC Religious Broadcasting Department shows that over half the population of adults in this country consider the church out of touch with life as lived by millions of people today. What could be viewed as the church's failure to communicate faith effectively has left a huge gap in both religious knowledge and experience within the lives of ordinary men and women. Religious broadcasting goes some way towards filling that gap, entering the homes of many who will never cross the threshold of a religious building or attend a ceremony. It has become a valuable bridge by which listeners are encouraged and persuaded to consider a spiritual side to their lives. Informing, discussing and debating religious issues, as well as hearing about religious influences upon the lives of famous or influential people, is an important part of helping people to accept faith as a normal and relevant part of modern life. The gloomy statistics informing us of the decline in church attendance in Britain are not reflected in the figures representing the millions who tune into Sunday morning religious broadcasting. If the BBC's statistics are to be believed, there appears to be a growing interest in the spiritual side of life and a desire to explore faith and spirituality. 'Good Morning Sunday' receives by far the highest proportion of those people and Don is considered the one person able to sustain and encourage that momentum.

What few skills he lacked at the outset of his time with 'Good Morning Sunday' the producers felt sure Don would quickly acquire. His strengths far outweighed his weaknesses. He had accumulated years of experience in Radio 2 broadcasting, was an avid listener to the station and knew his audience well. His personality was vibrant and consistent; his faith came over as solid and immovable. He was a layman with none of the encumbrances of being an official representative of institutionalized religion. He was up-front about his strong beliefs, quite able to talk openly about them and equally prepared to listen to those with differing opinions.

Whilst somewhat cloistered in Catholicism Don was happy to have his experience broadened. He was well aware of his initial lack of knowledge of other Christian denominations and other religious faiths but quickly came to view 'Good Morning Sunday' as a springboard from which he could confidently dive into new areas of religious knowledge and experience. He knew that his heart would always remain in the faith and denomination of his childhood but was open to exploring new and different ground in order to embrace the diversity of his listening audience. And the producers recognized in Don a quality that they valued above all others—his love of people. From the outset he thrived on the contact that he had with listeners, whether in person or through their letters, displaying a genuine interest and concern for them as individuals.

It was Don's natural charisma, wit and charm that finally won over the most doubting of listeners. Even during his three-week trial period he had generated considerable negative mail which continued after the announcement of his permanent appointment. The criticisms of his sense of humour, his Birmingham accent and his Catholic standing failed to concern Ernie Rea for one minute. He remained unwavering in his defence of Don and confidently extolled all the positive dimensions that he had brought to 'Good Morning Sunday'. Don himself was more saddened than upset by such criticism. Anyone who was so blinkered as to think that God only hears the prayers of those who are either Protestant or born with a Surrey accent was, in his opinion, to be pitied rather than chastised. As for the criticisms of his sense of humour, he had spent thirty years encountering those who either loved or hated it and was not going to be shattered by a few more critics along the way.

Not all his critics abandoned the programme; many stayed and one even wrote twelve months later to apologize for her unkind words, adding how much she was now enjoying the show. Don is never afraid of facing criticism and regularly reads out letters of complaint against himself. He is however concerned not to offend and quick to make amends for any unintentional hurt or pain that he may have caused. He is a sensitive, caring person with a tremendous capacity to empathize with his listening audience. It is this quality that remains his strength and the single most important factor responsible for the enormous popularity of the programme.

Letters from 'Good Morning Sunday' listeners have always been valued by the production team and frequently used as a barometer by which to gauge the impact of the show. Don's appointment generated an enormous response, both negative and positive but, since that time, the volume of mail received week by week has continued to grow. Don not only receives large numbers of letters requesting personal dedications and the promotion of religious events but also attracts a great deal of response relating to the wide range of topics covered in his handling of religious news and his weekly interviews with guests. Don thrives on what have become mini-debates across the air waves whereby he encourages individuals to have their say on issues relating to religion, faith and church. He has the rare ability to establish with Radio 2 listeners a relationship, based on trusted friendship, in which even the most doubtful find the confidence to express an opinion. Others, of course, need no such help or encouragement and make their feelings clearly heard. Whatever the opinion or the degree of feeling with which it is expressed, Don fully accepts them as individuals. These debates quickly gave birth to the Maclean catchphrase: 'let the laity have their saity!' and they have covered a wide range of topics in the last five years. The subjects have varied considerably: major issues such as the priesting of women and much lower-key concerns such as sharing God's peace by shaking hands in church services have each attracted thousands upon thousands of letters. Don has been surprised by both the breadth of opinions expressed and the degree of feeling with which they are aired. Some he has found interesting and intriguing; others simply unbelievable. 75 per cent of the people who contributed to the debate on the sharing of the peace in the service of Holy Communion stated that they did not want to be part of it. One lady actually wrote, 'I come to church to praise God, not to be friendly!'

Other letters have a much lighter and more humorous content and feed his comedian's heart! Don thrives on listeners' funny experiences of religion and church and delights in reminding his audience of his personal conviction that God laughs too. His advice to one listener (whose church organ was out of action) to accompany hymns with a comb-and-paper band was met with another's warning against it. This man relayed the story of his congregation's apparent attempt at such accompaniment—which resulted in a church full of dandruff! Some of the cleverest and funniest of letters came during discussion surrounding the advertising campaign launched by the Church of England. Don revelled in the dozens of letters describing Britain's wayside pulpit slogans. Among his personal favourites remains the church who took full advantage of its location alongside a private hospital by erecting a poster saying, 'Don't waste time, come in here for your FAITH lift.'

Current religious and church affairs have always lent themselves to debate but the feedback received from the popular interviews have been equally controversial in their nature. Even the future announcement of one particular guest brought in strong reactions from some listeners. When Don informed folk that Hugh Pinnock, UK head of the Church of Jesus Christ of the Latter Day Saints, more commonly known as the Mormon Church, was to be a future guest on the programme, the department received some of the most reactionary mail it had ever encountered. And the most fierce and disparaging came from individuals within the established Christian denominations!

Whilst the skills and techniques of interviewing were one area at which Don initially had to work very hard, the fruits of his labours have become clearly evident. As an ordinary layman himself he frequently asks his guests the kind of questions many listeners sitting at home long to ask. Occasionally he risks revealing his own naivety, especially on matters of theological importance but at these times such weakness actually becomes a strength. Many listeners, similarly limited in their understanding of theology, appreciate a layman's approach to a subject; the clear and simple explanations given may illuminate aspects of religion and faith that have previously escaped their understanding.

Don's guests have ranged from archbishops to comedians and include leading figures in the world of church, politics, literature, science, show business and sport. Whoever he is interviewing, he remains the same. In his five or more years as presenter he has interviewed over two hundred guests. Many have been both fascinating and thrilling to meet, others surprising—and some disappointing. A few have had a lasting impact upon Don. One he singles out more than any other—Joni Eareckson Tada. Injured as a teenager in a diving accident, Joni has lived her life confined to a wheelchair with all her limbs paralyzed. Her story of pain, suffering and the struggle to come to terms with her disability has been told to millions through books, broadcasts and her own lectures. Don has been privileged to speak with Joni on two occasions and remains deeply moved by her faith, her courage and her triumph in the face of adversity. When Joni spoke her whole face radiated the love of God and she left no one in any doubt that for her, God was a very real person with whom she and anyone else could have a relationship. Meeting her has been both a privilege and an inspiration for Don.

There have been very few of his near two hundred guests whom he hasn't enjoyed meeting but he admits to feeling most relaxed when dealing with friends and colleagues from his own world of show business. Don is unaffected by the fame and fortune that sometimes masks the true individual behind the public image and he often succeeds in uncovering the real person. He feels a very strong affinity with those in the business who share his passion for speaking about their faith and especially enjoys their appearances on 'Good Morning Sunday'. Don is full of admiration for people such as Cliff Richard—who was one of his first guests after he had officially taken over from Roger Royle—and Dana, who have spoken out and stood firm for their faith throughout the many years of their showbusiness careers. In recent years Don has enjoyed working and identifying with the organization set up especially for linking Christians in entertainment.

'Good Morning Sunday' is essentially teamwork, with Don presenting the results of several people's expertise. As a department the team enjoy good working relationships, all of which helps the creativity and smooth running of the programme and there is little doubt in the minds of producers, researchers and assistants as to the major contribution that Don makes towards team happiness. He gives of himself fully in every aspect of the job and is both loved and respected by all who work alongside him. The production team has grown in size from three to ten people over the last eight to ten years. As a full team they meet together five or six times a year in order to reflect on past programmes and plan ahead for the future. It is here that ideas and suggestions are tossed around. The final decisions are usually the result of several individuals' input and creativity. Don makes a valuable contribution at these times and has been the inspiration behind some of the programme's most successful ideas. Each week those responsible for the production of the following Sunday's show will be in regular contact with each other, Don being the one consistent member of the weekly team. When guests are unavailable for a live interview on the day, time has to be programmed in to visit them and record the interview in advance. During the early part of each week the mailbag is read, dedications and information spots are sorted, music selected, Bible readings chosen, research briefings prepared and interviews scripted. By the Thursday Don receives all the information he requires for the Sunday show through the post. He then spends most of Friday going through the material in detail, familiarizing himself with the order, writing his links between records, as well as gathering items for the writing of the prayers.

The inclusion of prayers was the very first personal contribution that Don made to the show but it wasn't many weeks before he had made the programme his very own. The biggest change to affect 'Good Morning Sunday' arrived at the start of the Gulf War in February 1991. Just five months after he had joined the programme, Frances Line, the then Controller of BBC Radio 2, allocated the programme an extra half-hour of air time, extending it to two hours, from 7a.m. to 9a.m. The main reason was to allow a religious programme to handle any traumas and atrocities that might have occurred in the Gulf during the night. In the event there were fortunately very few that required the kind of serious attention first anticipated. However, the extra half-hour provided Don with the opportunity to shape the programme around his individual style and he succeeded in a manner that far outweighed the expectations of all concerned. Two of the simplest ideas provided a hugely successful structure to the extra time. The Dawn Chorus formed and continues to unite all lovers of well-known and traditional hymns in a nationwide choir whilst the Sunday School quiz offers rewards to one of many listeners who weekly scan the Bible in search of an unidentified passage read by Don himself. Whilst never used for its original purpose, additional time for 'Good Morning Sunday' met with the approval of Radio 2's controller and has remained an extremely popular part of the programme.

The second half-hour of the show introduces the first and shortest of the weekly guest spots which are always taken by a leader of one of the church's established denominations. During his early months with the programme Don inherited the popular Anglican bishop of Southwark, the Rt Rev. Jim Thompson, as a regular occupant of this reflective, meditative slot. At first Don was quite nervous about speaking with the hierarchy of the church and completely unaware of church etiquette. With the help of his production team and the support of Bishop Jim as an experienced broadcaster, Don gradually learned to relax and quickly gained in confidence. By the time the Rt Rev. Roy Williamson took over the spot, a year or more later, he felt in complete control, not only in the way he conversed with the clergy but also in his decision to change the direction of the three or four minutes of chat following their thought for the day. Don now regularly selects a topical item of news that may have serious or controversial repercussions for faith and church. Many of his early guests who include members of all Christian denominations as well as a Jewish rabbi, are faced with the challenge of discussing current issues before a captive audience. It is not Don's intention to catch them out or deliberately make their interview difficult but simply to address matters that affect ordinary people in everyday life. Over a period of five or more years working with Don in this way Bishop Roy Williamson has seen a tremendous growth in confidence in the way he handles this interview time on the programme. In speaking of Don he says:

> *Two things impress me about the way in which Don Maclean conducts an interview. Firstly, he is genuinely interested and excited about the subject in hand and secondly, he really listens to what you are saying.*

Bishop Roy knows just how important these early-morning discussions are to listeners. As he meets people in his diocese and the wider country continual reference is made to the programme and especially the interviews with church leaders.

Meeting a wide range of religious leaders has been a tremendous learning experience for Don and one which he considers himself privileged to have received. Men and women of every conceivable denomination have given him new insights which have enriched the depths of his spirituality and he remains truly grateful for that.

Inviting guests onto the programme remains a valuable part of 'Good Morning Sunday' but, in the last few years, going out to meet listeners has become an increasingly important policy of the whole Radio 2 network. Several programmes and presenters have ventured forth 'on the road' and 'Good Morning Sunday' has been part of that development. For the last five years the team has visited a number of different venues with their 'Summer Special's, meeting face to face with thousands and thousands of regular listeners. The phenomenal number of people who rise early and travel considerable distances to be part of the broadcasts never ceases to amaze Don and the production team. Whilst many who remain listening at home express their preference for the statutory two hours' studio programme, there is never any doubt as to the pleasure experienced by the thousands who are able to share in the outside broadcast. Weeks of research and advance preparation go into bringing together musicians, local church leaders, congregations and special guests for the one-hour recordings. They are frequently at the mercy of the weather but, if enthusiasm and numbers are at all relevant to an event of this kind, they can only be rated as hugely successful. Having a presenter who can skilfully handle lively, enthusiastic audiences has been a major contributory factor to that success. Don simply thrives on the experience and regularly captures the hearts of his audience with his very special charisma. His love of and skill in handling people is more clearly demonstrated at these times than at any other.

The 'Summer Special's are just one group of many programmes recorded outside the BBC's Manchester-based studio. These have included very special, personal highlights for Don in the last five years, taking him into situations and places that he never dreamed he would have the privilege to visit. Attendance at the 1993 Remembrance Day service in Ypres and celebrating Easter 1995 in Rome stand out as two particularly moving occasions, not least because of his personal interest in both World War I history and Roman Catholicism. The live broadcast from St Peter's Square in Rome let Don join pilgrims from all around the world as they gathered for the traditional Easter blessing from Pope John Paul II. Don met with members of the Vatican staff, interviewed Cardinal Edward Cassidy and the Pope's Latin

Secretary, Fr Reginald Foster and heard what it is like to live and work in Vatican City. Italian tenor Luciano Pavarotti, a committed Catholic himself, joined Don as his guest for the second half of the programme. It is a day firmly engraved upon his memory.

The annual gathering of evangelical Christians called Spring Harvest was another special event, one that changed Don's understanding of evangelical Christianity. Rarely before has he encountered such enthusiasm and commitment towards the Christian faith as well as such lively, vibrant worship. Don discovered among the people there a deep sincerity and determination to make Christianity understood and relevant to life in an atmosphere of great informality. His three visits in the last five years have all been very special occasions.

Working Christmases are a regular feature of Don's hectic lifestyle especially since he has taken part in pantomime for over thirty years. The pantomime season brings additional pressures to several weeks of the year, especially in light of the current trend to stage two performances each Sunday. A total of four pantomime performances as well as presenting 'Good Morning Sunday' in one weekend leaves very little time in which to breathe, let alone sleep. Despite needing very little sleep Don would be forgiven for wanting a rest on Christmas Day but, since the start of his time with 'Good Morning Sunday', he has not only worked each Christmas Day but, on three occasions, invited the entire production team to record the early morning show live from his Solihull home. Salvation Army bands and songsters, bellringers, family, friends, neighbours, bishops and celebrities all pile into the Maclean homestead from 7.30a.m. onwards. The Pebble Mill engineers arrive at 6a.m. whilst some of the production team simply find it easier to stay the previous night. One year the team went to record part of the midnight mass from Don's home church, Our Lady of the Wayside, in Solihull. The whole event is just sheer delight to Don; one enormous party shared with his millions of listeners.

The Christmas broadcasts have been very special times for thousands of listeners but especially those living alone. One widower, alone for the first time in fifty-two years, made his own pilgrimage to Don's local church, having heard him mention that he would be attending mass following the live Christmas morning broadcast. Don was sitting with his family close to the front of the church during the administration of Holy Communion when he became aware of a figure standing in front of him. When he looked up he saw a small elderly man standing there silently, overcome by emotion, with tears streaming down his face. Don instinctively put his arms around him but the man was quite unable to speak. After a short while he made his way to the back of the church and stood by the crib. Don followed him, to learn that he had been away from church for over twenty years and unable to go anywhere in the last eight years due, to his wife's illness. He later wrote to Don explaining:

> When I went to the crib to ask for solace, I was not alone because I felt the arm of an angel around me to share my grief. That angel was no less that Don Maclean. You will never know the comfort that you gave me that day. You are wholly responsible for bringing me back to the church although spiritually I never left it. So amid my tears I felt happiness too.

'Good Morning Sunday' has come to mean a great deal to Don over the last five and a half years. What initially appeared to him as one crazy idea is now a very, very important part of his life. He tells journalists, 'What I am really trying to say on the programme is, "God loves us". I want to be very basic about belief in God. I look upon the programme as an opportunity to encourage people to think about religion and think about God.' He has tried to be more than just interesting and informative in supplying humour and entertainment as well. Don dislikes what he calls 'po-faced religion' and feels sure that there will be far more laughter in heaven than we encounter on earth. Part of what he achieves in his role as presenter is to give people a taste of heavenly laughter on earth and in so doing he accomplishes a lot more besides. 'Good Morning Sunday' has provided many of its listeners with insight and inspiration, help and hope. It gives them a platform on which to explore and express their own thinking about faith in God; many of whom are doing so for the first time in their life. It means different things to different people but there continues to be an ever-increasing number who choose to tune into Radio 2 regularly on a Sunday morning and Don is genuinely delighted to have each one of them.

15

Broadening Horizons

Don Maclean acknowledges that since working on 'Good Morning Sunday' he has been introduced to a whole new way of thinking about God, faith, Christian denominations and other religions. However, throughout what has been an intense period of exploration and learning, nothing has seduced him away from Christianity and especially Roman Catholicism. The roots of his faith lie deeply embedded in the church of his childhood and remain beyond the strength of any temptation to uproot or any enticement to change. Consistent spiritual nourishment has ensured an unwavering faith though he readily admits that in recent years that faith has been deepened and enriched through his work with 'Good Morning Sunday' and the wider religious broadcasting scene. One very important outcome of this experience is that he now chooses to call himself first and foremost a Christian rather than a Roman Catholic. The emphasis has not diluted his love for, or convictions about his mother church but affirms his desire to be seen as part of a wider Christian community and not just one denomination within it.

Even with his increased knowledge and experience of many different Christian denominations Don remains deeply passionate about his Catholic identity and eternally grateful for what he considers a strong and positive start to his faith. The appeal of Catholicism for him extends far beyond simply the security and familiarity of his childhood years—even without these early beginnings he feels sure that his own spiritual journey would have eventually led him to the Roman Catholic Church. His theatrical spirit is drawn and nourished by the richness of its worship and his faith is sustained by the disciplines expected of a committed member of this denomination.

The rigours of the faith are very important to him and he struggles to understand those who may choose to claim their Catholicism in name only. Being part of a regular worshipping community, including attending mass and confession, remains the focal point of his week, that brings him before God on a regular basis. His childhood experience was of the weekly mass said in Latin and he remains one of many who were saddened by the introduction of English in the service brought about by the Second Vatican Council in 1968. Don feels that some of the other relaxations in personal disciplines introduced at the same time have taken away a sense of identity amongst Catholics, sometimes undermining their security. As he is a vegetarian, fasting from meat on a Friday was not a particularly big issue for Don but he always felt that this simple practice provided a strong corporate identity which is now lacking among Catholics. Other changes—such as the participation of the members of the congregation in the mass through the distribution of consecrated bread and wine and the reading of set Bible passages—he has warmly welcomed. His church, like any other, is facing the challenge of making itself understood in the modern age. It seeks to encourage and equip its members, building on its strengths and wrestling with its weaknesses. Don recognizes its imperfections but remains totally committed to working from within as a member and is proud to claim it as his spiritual home. The Roman Catholic Church is equally proud to own Don.

Don's exposure to other Christian denominations came about immediately he started to present 'Good Morning Sunday'. It was sudden and the magnitude of it took him by surprise. Because he was a comedian, it was always Don's instinct to give people different labels and he was equally prone to doing so in a religious sense. The production team had warned him about his need to be sensitive and aware of other faiths and denominations but it wasn't until he actually came face to face with the situation that he realised just how cloistered he was in Catholicism. His entire knowledge of Christianity had come from within this one denomination. Other than at the occasional wedding and christening—and attendance at church parade as a Cub Scout—he has hardly ever worshipped outside his tradition, let alone engaging in a conversation about faith with a member of another denomination or religion.

Within just a few weeks huge quantities of new information was being thrown at him from all directions. He encountered people from different faiths as well as people from different denominations within the Christian faith and it wasn't long before he was realizing there were different emphases and traditions within the same denomination. It was a totally unexpected encounter, throwing him into a cauldron of new ideas, information and experiences. It was the responsibility of his researcher, Rosemary Foxcroft, to brief and prepare him for many of his new encounters especially in regard to the wide range of people he had to interview. She very quickly recognized the need to help him be more open-minded about the individuals and situations that he faced and has found the results richly rewarding. Some of the seemingly most incompatible guest/presenter combinations have turned out to yield hugely successful interviews. She says that Don is teachable in most things and has got a lot easier to brief over the years. She finds him very relaxed and easy-going to work with and admits that, on occasions, he even makes *her* laugh!

Much of what Don encountered in his early days was pleasantly enlightening. Senior clerics in the Anglican Church and ministers from the nonconformist traditions had previously been distant, unknown quantities. His discovery of them as perfectly ordinary men and women, willing and able to relate to all aspects of the everyday lives of his listening audience, was a revelation in itself. The Roman Catholic hierarchy always seemed so much more distant than for example, the bishops in the Anglican Church and he counts it as one of his greatest privileges to have interviewed Archbishop George Carey on several occasions. Don considers him to be one of the most holy of men that he has ever met. There have been very few occasions on which he hasn't felt able to express himself honestly before these church leaders or ask a question that may have appeared overly simple or controversial. Don has experienced an openness, warmth, deep sincerity and acceptance from them as they have shared his desire to make faith accessible and relevant to the listeners. They have taught him a lot about respect and tolerance within religion for which he remains grateful.

Learning about and in some cases experiencing their different styles and forms of worship has also been enriching. Whilst his personal preference will always lie within the Roman Catholic tradition, Don is glad to have the opportunity to join in fellowship with a wider spectrum of Christian worshippers. He remains firmly convinced that worshipping together as Christians can only serve to increase mutual knowledge and understanding of one another and be a preparation for the day when all shall be united in heavenly worship!

Worshipping at Spring Harvest with thousands of Christians from a wide range of different denominations provided him with a glimpse of what that might be like. Toni also found the experience thoroughly enjoyable. Simply to be among such unashamed, enthusiastic worship in an ecumenical setting was something she had never previously experienced. The informal, modern and almost 'showbiz' style of communication appealed to them both and they saw first-hand what kind of impact it had upon the people there. It also had an impact upon Don and brought a whole new understanding of the Christian charismatic movement and their emphasis on the Holy Spirit. He has since become very interested in the growing charismatic movement within the Roman Catholic Church.

As well as encountering a wide range of different styles of Christianity and worship, Don has also been faced with differing academic and theological opinions though he finds this whole area rather offputting. He describes himself as 'a bit of a peasant' when it comes to faith, preferring to keep his beliefs as simple as he possibly can. He's sure in his own mind of what he believes and has little desire to question it. He considers himself as a Christian who accepts that the way to God and eternal salvation is through Jesus Christ. He encourages himself with the knowledge that Jesus himself kept matters simple, often telling stories and speaking in parables in order to communicate simply and effectively to the people around him. He sees no real need to challenge what has provided him with a secure framework for living and a relationship with God and knows that his life would be much poorer without it. Don has never wandered away from his faith although he did go through a period, in his early twenties, of delving deeper into what he believed. It was a difficult time and an experience which he has no desire to repeat. Whilst he is happy to learn as much as he can and share in the experience of others, he chooses not to ask probing questions simply for the sake of it. He doesn't pretend to be a theologian, either privately or publicly and feels sure that those radio listeners who wish to enter into theological discussion and debate would be better served by Radio 4. The role of 'Good Morning Sunday' is not to dispute the components of faith but more to inform, encourage and aid listeners in their own exploration of matters of faith. It is with this in mind that Don presents the programme and does so with great sincerity.

'Good Morning Sunday' has opened doors for Don into a wider world of religious broadcasting, part of which has included a number of appearances on BBC 1's 'Songs of Praise'. The person who first invited Don onto this new ground was John Forrest, an ex-producer of 'Good Morning Sunday' before Don's time. Over recent years the BBC has developed a bi-media approach to their religious broadcasting on the production side of the work and this has also been reflected in the selection of presenters. The presenter who most frequently sits in Don's seat on 'Good Morning Sunday' during holiday periods is Pam Rhodes, a familiar face on 'Songs of Praise'.

She welcomed the opportunity to dabble in radio broadcasting and recalls her first week in Don's seat quite vividly. She felt exceptionally nervous having never done any radio work before and was well aware of Don's reputation in 'the business' as a true professional. Having appeared in the Black and White Minstrels herself early on in her own career (although never actually with Don) she had worked with many artists who knew him well and had spoken highly of him as a person and performer. She knew from her own listening that he came across as a sincere, committed and caring person and she also loves his use of humour on the programme. Nobody was more helpful to Pam on that first occasion that Don himself. She phoned him up to ask numerous questions and he took the time and trouble to answer each one whilst at the same time supplying lots of encouragement and support. Don was also the first to ring her up following her first broadcast in order to say 'Well done!' They both thoroughly enjoy 'sitting in each other's seat', complementing each other in style and personality and Pam fully recognizes the enormous talent and skill that Don has brought to 'Songs of Praise'.

John Forrest's choice of Don was not a simple matter of following this BBC bi-media policy but a conscious decision to engage both those skills as a light entertainer and his commitment to faith. From time to time 'Songs of Praise' seeks

to combine popular activities and special events with a celebration of faith, in an attempt to bridge the gap between
church and everyday life. Many of these programmes are
filmed away from church premises, in concert halls, theatres,
even on board a ship or in an airport terminal and quite often
in the open air. In such circumstances Don becomes a very
obvious choice as presenter. It is in this sort of setting that he
has learned his trade and is most able to do what he does best
of all—make people laugh. As a producer John Forrest
welcomes the opportunity to explore the boundaries between
humour and faith and Don is his greatest ally in this quest.
Being thoroughly drenched in a background of comedy, Don
communicates faith in the only way he knows how: through
laughter.

Traditionally faith and laughter sit uncomfortably with
each other; over the years an enormous gulf has come between
the world of entertainment and church. Whilst high art forms
have been considered very suitable for religious communication, light entertainment—and particularly the world of
comedy—have been dismissed as frivolous, flighty and
inappropriate for people of devout faith. The church appears to
communicate a powerful message saying, 'Thou shalt not
laugh—and especially not in worship!'

As a result of such strong attitudes many artists within the
world of light entertainment have been unwelcome and
misunderstood by the church; even where they may have found
a degree of acceptance, some have been encouraged to seek a
way out of their profession because of its 'unsuitablility'. Few
churches appreciate the God-given gifts and skills of such
performers or encourage them in this particular calling. In this
respect Don remains very grateful that his spiritual home is one
where laughter has not been completely erased. Whether this is
directly attributed to its Irish influence or the easy integration of
faith and lifestyle within the Catholic Church, he's not sure but
his experience has been quite positive and perhaps has been

one of the reasons why he has managed to sustain his faith as a performer. Not only has he found encouragement and acceptance but, ever since attending church as a young child, he has come to expect the priest to stand up in the pulpit, perhaps say something funny and get a response from his 'audience'. As far as Don can see, the role of a priest on Sunday comes very close to what he himself does on many a Saturday in a club or theatre. Both are in the art of communication and performance. There can be little more dramatic than someone dressed in fancy costume (albeit clerical robes), elevated in a pulpit, trying to get through to a congregation.

Don is convinced that humour has a valuable part to play in communicating faith. Humour undoubtedly makes people relax and it demands some kind of response. Generally speaking, people remember what they laugh about. In his own experience Don has found that when priests attract his attention through humour he is far more able to retain the message that follows. Jesus himself held huge crowds of a mixed age-group of people. Thousands upon thousands of men, women, children and babies gathered regularly for long periods of time to listen to the great Master of communication. Don feels sure that Jesus used humour and stories in order to gain the attention of the people and succeeded in delivering some life-changing words in the process. He feels saddened by the fact that the church as a whole appears so reluctant to display *any* humour and continues to frown upon those who have a natural ability to laugh at life.

Don, as a comedian, instinctively looks at the funny side of the whole of life and that includes work, leisure, faith, topical issues of the day, family, friends and all aspects of relationships of every kind, including sex! He finds the fact that people, especially Christians, go out of their way to avoid even acknowledging sex, let alone talking and laughing about it, quite funny in itself. Humour has become such a natural and spontaneous part of his personality that he rarely stops to analyze what he is doing and often feels very hurt by those who accuse him of being insincere because of it. He never tells a joke with intended hurt or malice and would never select material that he wouldn't use in the company of his own mother, wife or children. In these days of intense political correctness and sensitivity to almost every group of people, at one time or another Don has been accused of being racist, sexist, insensitive and insincere. Twenty years ago he could rattle off a whole string of gags that would never cause the slightest flutter of offence but today the same material would generate an over-whelming response of antagonism.

Due to the ever-changing attitudes in society there are jokes that he no longer uses but he still finds this whole area a potential minefield, especially in the Christian circles in which he is increasingly moving. He sometimes wonders if some Christians ever laugh about anything and fears that heaven might end up being an incredibly boring place to be. Over the years millions of people have laughed at the sight of someone slipping on a banana skin. When considered in the cold light of day the reality of that scenario is far from funny but laughing at it is not intended to ridicule or cause further pain to that unfortunate person. In reality the opposite is quite likely as the laughter more often than not stimulates a response of immediate action and sympathy. Many have jumped to rescue someone from an unexpected and unfortunate slip or fall whilst simultaneously splitting their sides with laughter; the two are not necessarily conflicting responses. In the same way, Don hopes that the blend of his humour and faith will spur on those with little or no faith to explore the spiritual life further and that those who already hold strong beliefs will be encouraged to relax and see a lighter side to their lives, including their faith. He is sure that churches will become better places for a little humour. He has no desire suddenly to become a different person when he walks into church; his humour goes with him. That doesn't mean that he doesn't take his faith seriously, on the contrary, nothing is more important to him, as he so readily tells his audiences in clubs, halls, theatres and homes up and down the country.

Some will always remain sceptical about the contribution that Don or any other comedian and light entertainer can make towards religious broadcasting and especially Christian worship but whilst such people may be lost statistics in the ratings, thousands of others have been won over through his unconventional approach. One very special 'Songs of Praise' in 1994 gained over 40,000 participants on the day of recording and millions more viewers when it was broadcast a few weeks later. The celebration of faith and football at Manchester United's Old Trafford ground on Sunday 24 September 1994 is a day that remains firmly engraved upon Don's memory.

The previous largest participating audience of 'Songs of Praise' had been earlier in 1994 when around 7,000 people turned up in one of Birmingham's city squares for the celebration of National Music Day. The emphasis on that day had been fun in church music and Don had played an important part in that broadcast too. But Old Trafford turned out to be something of quite different proportions. Producer John Forrest had hoped for an audience of around 7–10,000, thinking that they would occupy one small section of the ground so that he could concentrate two or three cameras in that area. Don mentioned it for several weeks on 'Good Morning Sunday' and encouraged his early morning 'Dawn Choristers' to apply for tickets and become members of the largest choir in the country. Thousands upon thousands of them did so and, in the event, the demand for tickets was worthy of a cup final. At one stage of the preparations over 40,000 tickets had been distributed by the BBC and there was a waiting list of nearly 10,000. Over 2,000 were recycled through a returns system and, on the day, 33,177 people went through the turnstiles. That number increased further when a production team of almost 70 people, the Band of the Royal Marines, a 400-strong choir and various special guests were added. It took 14.8 miles of cable, 112 microphones, 8 cameras, 63 monitors and 74 rolls of video tape to make broadcasting history. The event was the biggest ever staged (as opposed to covered) and received front-page national press coverage the following day. The mixing of two great passions, football and faith, generated an atmosphere of infectious warmth on a windy and chilly autumn day. In the words of Liverpool supporter and specially invited guest, Stan Boardman, 'It's the only match of the day where everyone is on the same side and there's only one winner—the goal is God.'

Greetings flooded in from Archbishops, Bishops, Cardinals, Archdeacons, Moderators and other senior church dignitaries from every conceivable denomination. The response from celebrities invited to appear as guests was equally overwhelming. They included Manchester City's Terry Phelan, ex-New Zealand international rugby player 'Inga' Tuigamala, singer Dave Willets, who was then appearing in *Phantom of the Opera* in Manchester, Bryan Mosley ('Alf Roberts' from 'Coronation Street'), athlete Phyllis Smith and a large number of the cast of the Newcastle-based children's programme, 'Byker Grove'. Don's task as presenter at the ground was to hold the whole event together on the day. His appearance on the final screened version of 'Songs of Praise' transmitted the following month, represented only a fraction of his efforts throughout the event. Pam Rhodes presented the thirty-minute programme whilst Don had the joy of holding together nearly 40,000 people for almost three hours during the adventurous process of filming. In the opening moments he ran out onto the pitch, up the steps of the temporary staging and announced to the enormous gathering, 'I feel like a lion thrown to the Christians.' It produced the immediate effect of laughter!

It was the biggest audience that Don has ever had to play to and he thrived on the whole experience. Having immediately struck up a trusted relationship with the multitude gathered, he was able to exercise the very important job of crowd control. The technical problems involved in recording were immense, not least the three-second sound delay experienced around the stadium during the singing of hymns and songs. But Don was required to lead the people into rapturous applause, banner-waving cheers, stillness, absolute silence *and* control a never-ending Mexican wave! At one stage he succeeded in encouraging all 40,000 to focus in a spirit of prayer, during which a very important link was recorded within the stadium. Many of the press commented on his achievements with compliments such as:

> *Don Maclean, dressed like a Butlin's Redcoat, managed the masses with ease, hushing them to silence for the solemn moments and leaping up and down and waving his arms when he wanted them to cheer for Christ.*

Producer John Forrest feels sure that Don is one of the very few artists around who combine a sincere faith, a charismatic personality, immense skills as performer and broadcaster and the capacity to face such an enormous challenge and succeed at it. His role at Old Trafford was critical to the success of the event and it would clearly have been difficult to have used anyone else. It will remain a personal triumph for Don—and God!—for many years to come. His own quote to the press was, 'The BBC did not fill this stadium, Manchester United did not fill this stadium—GOD filled this stadium.' And Don Maclean was happy to be one of that number singing, amongst many other things, 'O when the Saints, O when the Saints go marching in...' Never before had men's, women's and children's emotions on a football pitch been swayed to such godly purposes.

Other special editions of 'Songs of Praise' that Don has been part of include a Panto Special recorded at Leeds City Varieties along with Dana, Cannon and Ball and Mary Millar (Rose in 'Keeping Up Appearances'). He has thoroughly enjoyed every one but has no desire to become a regular presenter of their more standard type of programme. There have however been further opportunities that have come his way within the religious broadcasting field.

Radio 2's World of Faith Week in 1993 was the first of three annual weeks devoted to looking more closely at faith and the ever-increasing range of religions practised in this country. On each occasion Don has been selected as presenter of the daily five-minute slots on Terry Wogan's 'Thought for the Day' and also used in a number of other documentary-style programmes broadcast throughout the week. Each year his own Sunday programme launches and closes the week, frequently incorporating interviews and discussions with senior leaders from different religions some of whom, like the Dalai Lama, have been international figures.

The first year was particularly demanding as Don had no detailed knowledge of any faith other than Christianity and much of that had been rapidly acquired since taking on 'Good Morning Sunday'. But it was a welcome challenge which served to broaden his horizons even further. Many Christians criticize both the religious broadcasting department and him as an individual for being instrumental in offering faiths other than Christianity a higher profile. Don feels obliged to remind such critics that the BBC are in the business of *religious* broadcasting, not *Christian* broadcasting. Whilst Christianity may still be the strongest religion in the country—a fact which is personally pleasing to Don—it is by no means the only one. He believes firmly that the root of religious prejudice is ignorance and events like World of Faith Week go a long way towards helping people understand each other's culture, lifestyle and beliefs. In many ways such understanding can help affirm an individual's own convictions and is often reminded of the fact that his own religious identity as a young Catholic child was made stronger through being in a non-Catholic school environment. The five-minute spots on prime-time programmes such as 'Wogan' provide insight and information to millions of listeners who might otherwise remain completely unaware of such matters. Don considers it an honour to be invited to be part of such an important week in the world of religious broadcasting.

Don's own profile as a presenter has been increasingly raised throughout the last five or more years since working with 'Good Morning Sunday'. In 1995 regional television also used him for a series of six local religious programmes. Nigel Gibbons, Head of Religious Broadcasting with the now Carlton Television company first met Don whilst visiting Jerusalem when 'Good Morning Sunday' were preparing for a live Christmas Day broadcast from Bethlehem. He knew of Don through the programme and enjoyed his relaxed and humorous style of presenting. He was also impressed with his immense knowledge of religious subjects and saw quite clearly that he was a committed Christian who was unashamed of his faith or Roman Catholic identity. Nigel was delighted when Don offered to discuss the possibility of working with the then Central TV company on a series of religious broadcasting programmes.

'Right or Wrong' selected a number of topical subjects and put together a two-minute film describing the issues surrounding each one. They ranged from the objections of one congregation to a fellow worshipper because of her decision to stock tarot cards and New Age-related items in her shop, to the difficulties surrounding terminally sick children at a local hospice. Each week two of these films were screened for audience and viewers, following which a team of just five or six people launched into discussion and debate about the subjects selected for that day. Don featured as one of three regular team members, along with Julian Pettifer and Anna Soubrey. He found it a taxing experience but also stimulating and rewarding, despite very little time in which to research the subject area, leaving him frequently having to think on his feet. Central TV were delighted with the result especially Don's part in it all and look forward to making another series in 1996.

On occasions Don has also received invitations to attend specific church functions, some of which have asked if he would preach. He never assumes a right to preach and is quick to make that clear to all who extend such invitations. But there have been times when he has agreed to address a church gathering although such occasions are rarely on Sundays or within the context of a service of worship, not least because Sundays continue to be one of his busiest working days. At these times Don remains consistently the same, a fun-loving comic who intuitively sees the funny side of life—including his faith. When he speaks he does so with laughter on his face and in his heart. It remains the only way he knows how to communicate and, as the boundaries of his work have been broadened, he blends and extends his love of God and of humour in an effort to reach the ever-widening horizons that God places before him.

16

Fifties and Facing the Future...

'Good Morning Sunday' may well have broadened Don's horizons spiritually and opened up a whole new realm of work for him but it has never drawn him away from his love of the wider world of entertainment and especially his passion for performing to live audiences. The pull of a live stage perform-ance remains as strong as it was thirty years ago. Pantomime and cabaret have never ceased to be an ongoing part of his years in show business and, after a break of ten years, he has recently returned to the summer season at a British seaside resort. These things alone can easily occupy up to two-thirds of his working year but he still finds time and space to fit in other different, new and challenging experiences. During the last few years Don has completed several comedy series for the BBC Light Entertainment's department on Radio 2, hosted and refereed thirty-two episodes of a BBC 1 day-time television quiz show and acted a part in the thirtieth production of a 'Carry On' feature film, in addition to his regular commitments of religious broadcasting, pantomime and cabaret and more recently the summer season.

Alongside his work he continues to make time with his now grown-up family a top priority. Whilst Rory is still living at home and is studying for a degree in sports science at Newman College, University of Birmingham, Rachel who married Guy Pattinson in 1991 lives and works just a short distance away from her parents' home in Solihull. Rory's ever-increasing rugby fixtures dominate Don's Saturday afternoons, as well as the occasional mid-week game for his university side whilst his own hobbies get conveniently slotted in and around his hectic schedule. Squash remains an important part of Don's life although recently he has been playing more for personal pleasure and fitness rather than serious competition. Whenever he can, especially during the summer months, he flies to and from his various engagements and finds no greater delight than spending a day off airborne. Occasionally he indulges in a whole week's holiday simply flying around the British Isles.

One of the most unexpected but welcome opportunities to come Don's way during this period has been the chance to play a part, albeit a very small one, in a full-length feature film. Hitting the big screen had always been a secret ambition of his but one he had long since dismissed as unobtainable. When in 1992 the producers of the famous 'Carry On' series decided on a major thirtieth production, entitled *Carry On Columbus*, he jumped at the opportunity to join members of the established team such as Jim Dale, Bernard Bresslow, June Whitfield as well as newcomers Maureen Lipman, Rik Mayall and Tony Slattery. In the film Don plays the part of a Spanish inquisitor, trying to detect Jewish infiltrators with a plate of ham sandwiches! As a strict vegetarian he was quite amused by the whole idea and told the press, 'I've always been a bit of a ham actor.' The making of the film in the famous Pinewood Studios was great fun and he remains delighted to have finally made his debut in one of a line of comedy classics.

Comedy on radio has also continued to feature strongly in his itinerary. The BBC Light Entertainment Department have welcomed many of Don's own ideas and offered him a role in their own creations too. Recently Don has completed a popular radio quiz show called 'Are You Sitting Comfortably?' As both presenter and quiz master he revels in the delights of posing challenging questions to a panel of showbusiness personalities, all of whom have had some connection with the world of children's entertainment. Not surprisingly the questions focus on TV programmes, films, comics, fashion and so on around the time of the contestants' childhoods. Bursting with humorous banter and razor-sharp quips, the programme took off to a hugely successful start in 1994 and was followed by further series in 1995 and 1996.

The last decade has seen a large increase in the number of quiz and game shows on both radio and television which, in turn, has generated a demand for hosts. Some critics adopt the opinion that comedians who have exhausted every avenue open to them as comics resort finally to the role of host in these programmes. There can however be little doubt that those experienced in the general world of Light Entertainment fit the bill as relaxed and light-hearted individuals who offer a spirit of informality and fun to a potentially tense competitive situation. In some respects Don developed such skills years ago in his holiday camp training ground. Helping people to relax and enjoy participating in the entertainment programme of a holiday camp follows much the same principle as hosting a quiz or game show. When in 1993 the BBC offered him the job of host and questionmaster for a daytime television programme called 'First Letter First' he didn't need persuading to accept.

The game was devised by Colin Johnson, a computer boffin who works for IBM in Warwick but Don's involvement was far more than presenter as he also played a big part in the writing of the hundreds of questions required for each pro-gramme. That was the first opportunity of its kind for Don since the production of ITV's 'Mouthtrap' back in the mid-eighties and after several years of having to keep talking into a microphone Don looked forward to being able to actually pause, smile and pull faces to a camera! Three contestants competed in answering crossword-type clues in order to win letters rather than points. One unique feature of the show was that instead of the normal procedure of simply pressing a buzzer in response to a question, contestants had to indicate the first letter of the answer to each question before they were given a chance to speak. The system quickly reduced the number of mumblings and hesitations often experienced by contestants in those circumstances. Don recorded thirty-two programmes throughout August 1993 prior to them being screened the following new year. An average of three million people watched the series, with one particular day scoring an unbeaten 4.1 million viewers, the highest ever recorded number for a daytime quiz show on BBC TV. More than one hundred individuals took the trouble to write in to say how much they had enjoyed it.

The BBC made plans to record a further series, with indications that there might be even more after that but, yet again, misfortune struck. A change of personnel within the game and quiz show department of the BBC introduced new thinking on the development of such programmes which served to cut short Don's attempts to revive his skills as a TV presenter. He still remains absolutely amazed that, yet again, a hugely successful television programme could be dropped but, unlike previous occasions in his career, the disappointment was very short-lived. Work was plentiful and even some of the most regular of commitments were bringing their own new challenges.

Whilst pantomime has remained a permanent familiar fixture in his diary for over thirty years, the 1994/5 season proved to be quite different. Having for many years played the loveable, 'silly-billy' youthful characters of Buttons, Wishee Washee, Idle Jack and Dopey Don whose primary role was to befriend the young children in the audience, Don knew that he didn't want to continue to pretend to be twenty when he clearly wasn't. It was becoming increasingly hard to convince even the children that he was a mere lad; sooner or later he'd have to change role. But whilst the invitation to play Dame Trott in *Jack and the Beanstalk* at Birmingham's Hippodrome didn't come as a complete surprise, it wasn't received with Don's usual spirit of enthusiasm. The decision was a big one and he didn't make it either quickly or lightly.

The traditional role is, in his opinion, one of the central characters in a pantomime and the move away from the eccentrically-attired, big-busted, 'old bag' mother-figure to a slightly more ambiguous and precarious female impersonator bothered him. He had no desire to follow the modern trends. In recent years the country has lost some of its finest perfectors in the art of playing dame in Les Dawson and Arthur Askey and Don was not at all sure that he could follow in their footsteps, least of all take up their mantle.

His own personal living role model was Frankie Desmond who had been Don's 'mother' in panto many times. Don had watched him perform for years and knew that this was the character that he longed to emulate. But ultimately his greatest fear, having enjoyed over thirty years of phenomenal success in pantomime, was failure. He had seen good comedians whose work he admired play dame badly and he had no intentions of doing that. Whilst it was highly unlikely that Don Maclean could ever fail to please his own Birmingham people, he was still determined to reach the high standards that he sets himself.

The invitation had come from the country's biggest name in pantomime production—Paul Elliot. Whilst he had never worked with Don previously he had always admired his work and was absolutely convinced that with his warmth of personality, smile, huge mouth and teeth Don had the makings of a great dame. Paul was very supportive throughout Don's doubts and deliberations and was delighted when he finally accepted the offer. As far as Don was concerned, if in his own mind he failed in the task, he knew that it would be the first and last time that he would ever appear on stage as a dame. There were a number of factors that helped him to reach the decision, not least that the Hippodrome line-up of stars proved to be quite spectacular, featuring personalities of stage, television, radio and the world of sport. Sharing the limelight with Don was star of television's 'Hi-de-Hi', Su Pollard. Ironically, Su's first ever pantomime was in 1977 at Wolverhampton where Don was top of the bill. On that occasion *she* had played dame. In Birmingham seventeen years later, Don was playing dame for the first time with Su as top of the bill.

The Hippodrome's production was billed as Britain's biggest pantomime. The all-star cast, topped by Don and Su, also included Kevin Lloyd (alias Tosh Lines of 'The Bill'), Ray Meagher (from 'Home and Away'), Radio 2's Judy Spiers, Gladiator Scorpio, Mallandra Burrows (better known as Kathy Tate in 'Emmerdale') and a relative newcomer to the world of show business, comic and singer Mike Doyle. It was a line-up guaranteed to produce a fine show and it was equalled by the amazing achievements of modern technology in the special effects. A spectacular sci-fi trip through space, a beanstalk that really did grow and the moving face and head of a giant that appeared to fill the stage left audiences and critics enthralled. Even the professional reviews raved about it. And they all singled out Don's debut performance as dame:

> *The Cadbury's sponsored extravaganza had everything—lavish sets, beautiful period costumes, a gala of special effects and lots of imaginations—all resulting in another huge success for the Hippodrome... the chocolate-covered Dame Trott kept proceedings moving along in a brisk and business-like manner with all the normal ingredients of local and topical jokes...*

Others showed their appreciation in even more graphic terms:

Maclean effortlessly demonstrates how a panto dame should be, a genuinely funny comic who never loses sight of the 'old bag' character. We could have savoured much more of him.

Don Maclean wore with style a dazzling array of bizarre, garish costumes you would expect for a panto dame and no one can deliver a large dose of comedy and gags better than he.

Naturally Don was pleased to receive such positive reviews following his doubts and anxieties. Apart from the painful experience of having to negotiate steps in high-heeled shoes, regularly remove vast quantities of upper body hair in order to wear dame-type costumes and adjust to not being able to see the lower half of his body, due to bosoms and enormous frocks, he survived the experience sufficiently well to agree to play dame in the 1995/6 Southampton production of *Jack and the Beanstalk* at the Mayflower Theatre. For many in the world of pantomime production Don Maclean has made the successful transition from Dopey Don to Dame Don and stands to become one of the country's finest and traditional performers of this age-old character. Paul Elliot himself said, 'I want to say to Don Maclean, "Sign here for life—as a dame!" In years to come he will become a classic dame in his own right and others will want to model themselves on him.'

On reflection 1994 turned out to be a year of several changes. It was during this year, following a gap of ten years, that Don made the welcome return to the world of the summer season. It was also a return to Clacton's West Cliff Theatre where he had topped the bill as an up-and-coming young artist in 1967. Over the years producer Francis Golightly has produced twenty-two shows at the Clacton theatre and remembers going to see Don's performance at that time. He recalls, 'Don Maclean was young, energetic, slick and extremely funny; he worked like a man who had been a professional for many years. I knew instinctively that he was going to be a star.' Don became the star of Francis' shows on several occasions and 1994 was no exception.

Twenty-seven years might have passed since that first performance but Don's love of a traditional summer show had not faded in any way. It was only the need to be home-based during the children's teenage years that had prevented him from continuing over the previous ten years. His last season had also been at Clacton's West Cliff Theatre in 1984, the year of Rachel's 'O' levels and also the summer during which he had learned to fly. Now that Rachel was married and Rory leading a quite independent life Don was happy to return to the prolonged summers away from home.

Francis Golightly attributes much of the success of the 1994 season to Don both as a performer and company member. His individual act is always well received but his willingness to work as part of a team bringing out the best in everyone is a quality valued by everyone involved. Francis said that Don never thinks of himself as a big star or of any greater importance than anyone else in the show. Many of the big seaside towns have stopped producing conventional revue-type shows, replacing them with one big top-of-the-bill name who proceeds to dominate the entire programme. Clacton is one of the few exceptions. Here the company work together, twenty-two artists working hard to provide an all-round excellent show producing reviews like: 'It's just good, clean family fun, always guaranteed to be bright, colourful, tuneful, funny and full of pace,' and 'Don Maclean is a consummate entertainer, whose comedy, singing and dancing are all of the highest order, with every pore oozing, not perspiration, but charisma.'

Seemingly Don wasn't the only Maclean oozing charisma during that 1994 season as it was there that his son Rory met Helen, one of the dancers, to whom he has since become engaged to be married.

Don couldn't be more delighted with his children's choice of life partners. He is especially proud of the fact that they have both chosen Christian marriage as a means of expressing their commitment to each other. But at the same time he is saddened by what he sees as the end of an era for him as a parent. His relationship with them is no less important but it has inevitably changed during these adult years of independence. Don clearly recognizes that it is a very natural progression—in many ways it is the fulfilment of all that he has hoped for them—but at the same time he hasn't found it easy and openly admits to struggling to let them go. For some time after Rachel got married he would feel quite upset at the slightest thing that reminded him of the fact that she had gone. Even the sight of her empty bedroom or having only to make three mugs of tea, instead of four, each morning were sufficient to cloud his day for a moment in the first few months following her marriage. In his wedding speech he announced to the gathering of friends and family that Rachel was only on loan to Guy—he wasn't really giving her away. Behind the smile was a grieving father, reluctant to let his daughter go. 'Devoted and doting father' is perhaps an understated description of Don Maclean. Whilst he is still coming to terms with the changes that having grown-up children bring to his life Rachel and Guy will present him with yet another new role during 1996 as they produce his first grandchild.

In sporting terms, Rory has probably provided Don with the greatest source of enjoyment and pride that a parent can know. Don's strong interest in rugby influenced Rory from the time he was first able to throw a ball—it was nearly always an oval-shaped one. The Sunday routine in the Maclean household rarely changed, beginning with attendance at family mass, followed by a trip over the fields to the nearby Solihull Rugby Football Club ground where father and son spent many hours negotiating moves, passes, tackles, conversion kicks and line-outs. It became clear to Don and coaches from the local club that Rory had talent and, given the right encouragement and help, he could progress far in the game. Not only has he been among the youngest in his age groups to represent his school and club first XV, in recent seasons he has also been selected to play for Warwickshire Colts, Midlands Colts and the Under 21's Scottish Exiles side (through the Maclean Scottish ancestry) and has had a trial for England Colts. One of the highlights of his career was to play in an England Colts Select XV against the Argentinian Youth XV. But as well as sharing in the successes of Rory's game, Don inevitably experiences the failures and disappointments too. Just a week after his selection for Scotland Under-21 squad Rory broke a leg and was laid up for most of that season. The distress experienced by both men on that occasion was far greater than the physical pain of the broken leg.

Don attends as many of Rory's games as he can, frequently organizing his diary around them and plays every move with him from the touchline. He struggles to find the words to describe adequately the emotions behind the experience of watching his son play rugby. It is a combination of agony and ecstasy, pain and passion, all rolled into one. It has the power to overwhelm and momentarily distort his perspective in life but the risks are worth taking for the sheer pleasure gained. More importantly for Don and Rory, at a time when many fathers and sons seem to be going separate ways, the world of rugby has become a strengthening bond in their relationship and the foundation of a firm friendship for which they will always remain grateful whatever future successes or failures the game may hold

Having a successful marriage and family life means more to Don than anything else. He and Toni celebrate thirty years of marriage during 1997. When speaking about their very successful partnership he is reluctant to suggest that what they have is at all unique or special and talks very philosophically about it saying, 'I don't see what the problem is. Life's very simple really. Every morning I do two things. Firstly I offer everything that I will think, say or do in that day to God and then I say to myself, "What can I do to make Toni happy today?" Now what could be easier than that?' And it really does appear that simple to Don. Anyone who has been in their company for more than half an hour is left in no doubt as to the commitment, love and affection that they have for one another. Both are clearly at their happiest when they are together. Toni continues to travel with him whenever she can and those who work with Don on a regular basis recognize that he is most content when she is around. When asked what he thinks the success of their marriage is, Don once more pleads naivety and simplicity, with an illustration from the world of catering. 'Marriage is a bit like being in a self-service restaurant. You pick up your tray, look around and decide upon your menu. You choose the things you want. You then sit down and enjoy your meal. What you don't do is start looking at what's on other people's plates and then decide you want that!' Don and Toni selected each other thirty years ago and have been determined and committed to enjoying each other ever since. Toni is quite content in her role as wife, mother and homemaker and undisturbed by the fact that her husband's culinary skills extend no further than making coffee and toast. She is quite delighted to be left to do the things she most enjoys doing, as is Don. They both find great security and affirmation within their clearly defined roles and have no desire to change what has brought them thirty years of happiness.

Whilst their arrangement does not project a popular image in these days of cohabitation and shared domestic responsibilities, it is one that Don firmly believes in and can testify to having proved enormously successful in his own experience. He is however quick to recognize that there have been very few pressures in their lives especially where money, which is recognized as the highest cause of marriage stress, is concerned. They have never had to worry about paying a mortgage, having a holiday or providing the next meal but neither are the Macleans greedy. Don was brought up by a father whose advice was always, 'Never own anything you can't afford,' so he never has. He has never borrowed money, other than a mortgage, they have only ever owned two houses in their entire lives, they always buy second-hand cars and Toni considers herself a great bargain hunter!

Don has no desire to acquire massive wealth or the status symbols coveted by many of his colleagues in the showbusiness world. His values and priorities are very different. He and Toni have spent a lot of money on keeping the family together and trying to provide an education that would help bring the best out in their children. Don considers his two luxuries to be his aeroplane, which doubles up as a means of transport for work and their holidays. At the end of the day he knows that money does not motivate him and never will. Even today the amount he is paid for a job will be one of the last factors to be considered in making a decision. He is certain that those most affected by the sudden acquisition of a lot of money are those who have had least and he doesn't consider himself to have ever been hard up or in great need. He remains extremely grateful for what he has been able to earn and sometimes embarrassed by the amount. Many years ago Arthur Askey advised him, 'Always be value for money, Don,' and he has always tried to be that. Working hard and giving of his best is very important to him. Should he ever fail to do so he would feel as if he were stealing.

Don Maclean is a hard worker in all areas of his life and his marriage, family, career and personal interests all bear the fruit of hard work and dedication but he sees no reason why that in itself warrants praise or attention. In Don's eyes it is his responsibility before God and towards the people with whom he lives and works always to give the very best of himself in all situations. And he considers himself extremely fortunate. Looking back over more than thirty years in show business he knows there have been disappointments and mistakes. With the experience of hindsight he thinks that leaving 'Crackerjack' was one of those mistakes but also knows that staying wouldn't have guaranteed him success at the top. He is also sorry to have left his agency Aza Artists when he did and recognizes just what a valuable relationship he had with Morris Aza. Part of him will always feel sad about the loss of successful television pro- grammes such as 'The Cheapest Show on Telly' and 'Comedy Connections'. but he has not allowed these memories to make him bitter. Mistakes can be turned into learning experiences and Don hopes that he has learned through these and other difficult times. But it is the positive memories that surface the fastest in his mind and among the happiest are the days with the Black and White Minstrels and also the years presenting 'Crackerjack'. It was during those years that he was stretched as a performer and his potential was truly explored. They were exhausting but very fulfilling years for him as an artist and provided a great deal of satisfaction.

Don sometimes questions whether his full potential has ever been fully explored and wonders if his time is yet to come. His work over the last few years within religious broadcasting and the Radio 2 scene have charged areas of him that make him think that there might still be a lot, lot more to come. How and when, he is not sure. His strongest ambitions remain firmly focused on his family who will always be the most important people in his life. He says that if, when he is dead and gone, he is remembered most as a man who has had a successful marriage and family life, he'll be content.

In career terms there are still one or two things that he would like to do if the opportunity comes his way. The idea of playing a religious character in a straight drama appeals to him and he would also like to find time to finish his novel so that it can be published. Religious broadcasting continues both to amaze and to excite him. There are still days on which he cannot believe that he is working in that department and remains convinced that it all came about by divine intervention!

'Good Morning Sunday' is no longer a job to Don; it's a ministry which he values more than anything else he has ever done. If only one person is helped to faith through his efforts he feels it will all have been worthwhile. In his mind, there can be no greater privilege than being used by God to bring others to faith. He's not sure what the future will hold but regularly prays 'Please show me if there is something else you want me to do' and waits patiently for God's guidance. He'd like to think he may still be presenting the programme in five years' time but fears that the audience may have grown tired of him long before then. Such fears are not shared by Ernie Rea, the Head of Religious Broadcasting at the BBC, who makes it quite clear that 'there are no plans to replace Don Maclean.'

Don would be irreplaceable to many people for many different reasons. Fellow 'Crackerjack' presenter Michael Aspel says that he is 'one of those utterly reliable, professional, versatile performers that the British entertainment industry used to rely on.' That era may well have passed but Don Maclean is still 'smiling through' and still popular in a much wider and very different world from the one in which he started out. He brings with him a wealth and a depth of experience in life and the world of entertainment. 'Good Morning Sunday' has clearly marked the beginning of a new and very important era in his life. When the time does come for him to leave, he will be missed by many. To thousands upon thousands of listeners Don Maclean remains an unashamed, sincere and committed Christian, transparently so, with the skills and personality to communicate a tremendous love of life and a tremendous faith, in the most natural, spontaneous and infectious way. He does so using every God-given gift within him—and especially his sense of humour.

Some significant dates in Don Maclean's life and career

1943   Born 11 March

1961   Entertainments manager at Northney, Hayling Island

1962-64 Birmingham Theatre School

1964   Summer season at Skegness' Pier Theatre

1964/65 Pantomime in Southampton at the Gaumont Theatre

1965   Summer season at Akegness' Pier Theatre

1965/66 Pantomime at Kidderminster Playhouse and Louth Playhouse

1966   Summer season at Felixstowe's Music Hall

1966/67 Pantomime at Weston-super-Mare's Knightstone Theatre

1967   Married Toni 11 February and went to Australia with her

1967   Summer season at Clacton's West Cliff Theatre

1968   Billy Cotton Music Hall - Live BBC Television

1968/69 The White Heather Club tour

1969   Rachel Heather Maclean born 19 March

1969   Summer season with The White Heather Club in Llandudno

1969/70 Pantomime at Bradford's Alhambra Theatre

1970   Summer season at Blackpool's North Pier Pavilion

1970   Two weeks in November at London's Palladium Theatre

1970/71 Pantomime at Oxford's New Theatre

1971   Club work in Australia during the British summer season

1971/72 Pantomime in Birmingham at the Birmingham Theatre

1972   Rory Gregor Maclean born 24 June

1972   Summer season at Blackpool's Opera House

1972   'Crackerjack'

1976/77 Pantomime at Wolverhampton's Grand Theatre

1977   Summer season at Scarborough's Futurist Theatre with the Black and White Minstrels

1977   Autumn recording of 'Maclean Up Britain' for Radio 2

1977   Made the decision to leave 'Crackerjack'

1979   Summer season at Torquay's Princess Theatre

1979   'The Cheapest Show on Telly'

1981   ITV's 'Super Savers'

1981/82 Pantomime at Birmingham's Repertory Theatre

1982   Summer season at Felixstowe's Spa Pavilion

1983/84 Pantomime at Swansea's Grand Theatre

1984   Falklands trip to entertain troops

1985   'Mouthtrap'

1985   Touring with stage play 'A Bedful of Foreigners'

1986   Touring with stage play 'Chase Me Comrade'

1990   'Good Morning Sunday'

1994   Pantomime at Birmingham's Hippodrome Theatre

1994   Summer season at Clacton's West Cliff Theatre

1995/96 Pantomime at Southampton's Mayflower Theatre

1996   Summer season at Clacton's West Cliff Theatre

INDEX